JOHN

BREAKING
INTIMIDATION

WORKBOOK

Breaking Intimidation Devotional Workbook
Copyright © 2008 by Messenger International

Published by: Messenger International, P.O. Box 888, Palmer Lake, CO 80133-0888.
All rights reserved. No portion of this book may be reproduced, stored in a retrieval system, or transmitted in any form or by any means —electronic, mechanical, photocopy, recording, or any other—except for brief quotations in printed reviews, without the prior permission of the publisher.

Unless otherwise noted, Scripture quotations that are unmarked (or marked NKJV) are taken from the NEW KING JAMES VERSION. Copyright © 1979, 1980, 1982 by Thomas Nelson, Inc. Used by permission. All rights reserved.

Scripture quotations marked AMP are taken from the AMPLIFIED® Bible. Copyright © 1954, 1958, 1962, 1964, 1965, 1987 by The Lockman Foundation. All rights reserved. Used by permission. (www.Lockman.org)

Scripture quotations marked KJV are from The Holy Bible, KING JAMES VERSION.

Scripture quotations marked NIV are taken from the HOLY BIBLE: NEW INTERNATIONAL VERSION®. Copyright ©1973, 1978, 1984 by International Bible Society. Used by permission of Zondervan. All rights reserved.

The "NIV" and "New International Version" trademarks are registered in the United States Patent and Trademark Office by International Bible Society. Use of either trademark requires the permission of International Bible Society.

Scripture quotations marked NLT are taken from the Holy Bible, New Living Translation. Copyright © 1996. Used by permission of Tyndale House Publishers, Inc., Wheaton, IL 60189. All rights reserved.

Scripture quotations marked The Message are taken from THE MESSAGE. Copyright © 1993, 1994, 1995, 1996, 2000, 2001, 2002. Used by permission of NavPress Publishing Group.

Scripture quotations noted TLB are taken from The Living Bible. Copyright © 1971. Used by permission of Tyndale House Publishers, Inc., Wheaton, IL 60187. All rights reserved.

WRITTEN AND EDITED BY:
Vincent M. Newfield
New Fields & Company
P. O. Box 622 • Hillsboro, Missouri 63050
www.preparethewaytoday.org

COVER, INTERIOR DESIGN & PRINT PRODUCTION:
Eastco Multi Media Solutions, Inc.
3646 California Rd.
Orchard Park, NY 14127
www.eastcomultimedia.com

Design Manager: Aaron La Porta
Designer: Heather Wierowski

Printed in Canada

TABLE OF CONTENTS

Quick Overview and Suggestions for Use v

CHAPTER 1   Your Place of Authority 1

CHAPTER 2   Imparted Gifts 17

CHAPTER 3   The Spirit of Intimidation 37

CHAPTER 4   The Spirit of Intimidation II 53

CHAPTER 5   Stir Up the Gift – *Power* 71

CHAPTER 6   Stir Up the Gift – *Love* 91

CHAPTER 7   Stir Up the Gift – *Sound Mind* 109

CHAPTER 8   Press On 129

Quick Overview and Suggestions for Use

Welcome to the *Breaking Intimidation Devotional Workbook*. It is a privilege to present to you this eye-opening, interactive study based on John Bevere's book and teaching series. Without question, we firmly believe that this curriculum is for such a time as this. It has been bathed in prayer from the start and is anointed by God to bring you into new levels of freedom from fear.

In this study, there are eight chapters that correspond to the eight DVD sessions. Each chapter is developed from one or more chapters in the *Breaking Intimidation* book and includes a series of soul-searching questions, an inspiring devotional, as well as an area to *Pen Your Progress* as you learn and grow each week.

Other Features to Look For in Each Chapter:

- **Encouragement from the Courageous** – inspiring quotes from heroes of the faith, both past and present, that add a unique perspective and help drive home the heart of the message.

- **Scriptures** – life-changing messages of truth and hope from God's Word. Nothing packs greater power to change your life than the strength of Scripture in the hands of the Holy Spirit!

- **John's Quotes** – key insights from the book and DVD sessions that reinforce the compelling principles of each chapter.

- **Make It Real** – creative assignments designed to help you defeat fear and cultivate faith in your everyday life.

Your journey toward *breaking intimidation* will also be enriched by a number of fascinating facts, heartfelt prayers and key definitions included throughout the study. Additionally, you can jot down the special insights the Holy Spirit reveals to you, along with your thoughts and feelings, in the *Freedom Notes* section at the end of each chapter. What God speaks to you is priceless and well-worth investing the time to write down.

WE SUGGEST YOU…

- **BEGIN AND END WITH PRAYER.** In every session, invite the Holy Spirit to teach you and guide you into all truth (see John 16:13). As you finish each chapter, ask Him to permanently seal in your spirit and soul what you have learned. It is amazing what He will reveal to you while you are studying—if you will only ask!

- **READ THE CORRESPONDING CHAPTERS** in the *Breaking Intimidation* book, watch the DVD teaching, and then complete the workbook lesson.

- **PACE YOURSELF** to complete each lesson during the week. You may do it as part of your daily routine or work on it two or three nights a week. Remember, there is no right or wrong way; this is your *personal* study with the Lord.

- **BE CONSISTENT.** Whatever time and place you decide to do your study, stick to it. If you fall behind, don't quit. *Press on* to the end. God will faithfully bless your every effort.

- **BE HONEST** with yourself and God as you answer each question. Knowing the truth of God's Word and the truth about yourself will bring freedom to your life that can be found no other way.

Open your heart to all that your heavenly Father desires to do in your life through this study. Allow Him to give you an eye-opening revelation of His intense love for you, the authority you have as a believer, and a growing understanding of the fear of the Lord. As you earnestly seek His face, He will hear you and deliver you from all your fears—igniting a fire of bold, fearless faith in you for the glory of His name!

"To have dominion in the earth requires a physical body. …**You** are the one with the body, and **you** have the authority! When your authority and God's ability get together, **all things are possible**."

—**Charles Capps**[1]

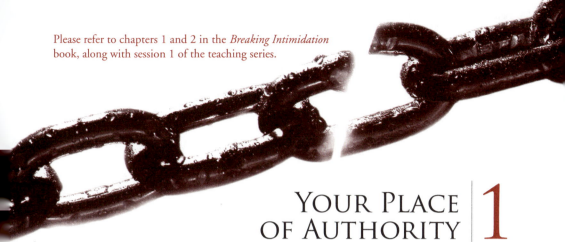

Please refer to chapters 1 and 2 in the *Breaking Intimidation* book, along with session 1 of the teaching series.

Your Place of Authority | 1

AUTHORITY

In the King James Version, the word *power* is often used in place of *authority*. Nevertheless, the original Greek word used is *exousia*, which generally means "permission, the right to exercise power; the power of rule or government (the power of one whose will and commands must be obeyed by others)."²

"…it is important to understand there is a *dwelling place* or position in the spirit that we hold as believers in Jesus. With this position comes *authority*. This authority is what the enemy wants. If he can get us to yield our God-given authority, he will take it and use it against us. This not only affects us but also those entrusted to our care."
—**John Bevere** (page 11)

1. As a believer, you have a specific *place* in the body of Christ over which you must stand guard. Why is it so important for you to know your place of authority? Name the two ways Satan can take your place from you.

_____
_____
_____
_____
_____
_____
_____

2. Although you are positioned in a physical body here on the earth, your *spiritual* position in Christ is very different. **Write out** and

hide in your heart these verses in Ephesians, revealing your powerful place *in Christ*:

EPHESIANS 1:20-21 – CHRIST IS SEATED *FAR ABOVE* EVERYTHING!

_____
_____
_____
_____

EPHESIANS 2:6 – YOU ARE SEATED *IN CHRIST*!

_____
_____
_____
_____
_____
_____

Encouragement from the COURAGEOUS

"God's masterpiece of creation, man, was made to be the master of the entire earth. …Adam and Eve had personal harmony with nature, open communication with God, peaceful dominion over the animals, the ideal physical bodies, intimate awareness of natural laws, and intimate response to spiritual laws. …With his God-like spirit, Adam and his family had the power to accomplish anything…."
—**Dennis Petersen**[3]

3. When God created Adam and Eve, He gave them dominion (power and authority) over *everything* on the earth. But when they sinned against God, they and all of mankind lost their rightful place of authority.

   a. What happened to everything under their authority as a result?

   _____
   _____

   Hint: Check out Romans 8:19-22

   _____
   _____
   _____
   _____

   Hint: Check out Luke 4:5-6

   b. Who gained man's place of dominion and authority?

   _____
   _____
   _____

c. Why was it vitally necessary for Jesus to come to earth in the form of a man who was born of a virgin?

___

4. First Corinthians 15:45 refers to Jesus as the *last Adam* who became a life-giving Spirit, restoring the dead to life. **Read** Romans 5:12-19, which shows the comparison and contrast between the first Adam and last Adam—our Lord Jesus. **Write out** the unique differences the Lord reveals to you.

> ### Encouragement from the COURAGEOUS
>
> "The only legal way to get into this earth with authority is to be born here. Even angels can't preach the Gospel in the earth. They don't have the authority. ...Jesus came by the legal entry, through birth. He had all the authority of a man. He lived as a man and was anointed with the Holy Ghost. He went before us and destroyed the devil's works. He went to the Cross, gave up His life, and became the supreme sacrifice...."
>
> —**Charles Capps**[4]

The First Adam

___

The Last Adam—Jesus Christ

___

5. Through His death, burial and resurrection, Jesus Christ took back the authority and dominion of the earth from Satan. In Matthew 28:18, He said, "**All** authority (all power of rule) in heaven and on earth has been given to Me" (AMP). He then commissioned us to go and make disciples of all nations.

   a. What is the connection between Jesus saying He has all authority and His commission to us to go and make disciples?

   Hint: **Check out** Ephesians 1:3 and Colossians 2:10

*If possible, **check out** this verse from the Amplified Bible. Visit www.biblegateway.com if you don't have a copy.*

b. **Write out** and **hide in your heart** the related power principle of Luke 10:19:

LUKE 10:19
_____
_____
_____

> He who *dwells* in the *secret place* of the Most High shall remain stable and fixed under the shadow of the Almighty [Whose power no foe can withstand].
> **—Psalm 91:1 AMP**
> [Italics added for emphasis.]

6. Are you living a roller coaster life of emotional and spiritual ups and downs? If so, God wants to help you get off the ride. How? By giving you a heart revelation of what it means to *dwell* in Him continually, not just visit Him once or twice a week. Slowly **read** and **meditate** on John 15:1-7.

   a. Who is the *vine* and what is His function?
   _____
   _____
   _____

   b. Who are the *branches* and what are their functions?
   _____
   _____
   _____

   c. Who is the *vinedresser* and what is His function?
   _____
   _____
   _____

   d. Ask the Lord to explain what it means to *dwell* in Him. Write what He reveals:
   _____
   _____
   _____

7. Without question, Satan seeks to undermine and destroy the body of Christ, and churches are one of his biggest targets. Who does Satan go after the most in local churches? Why? What should this prompt you to do?

Hint:
Check out 1 Timothy 2:1-2 and Hebrews 13:17

_____
_____
_____
_____
_____
_____
_____
_____
_____
_____
_____

8. According to James 3:1, why should people who desire to be pastors and teachers of God's Word be cautious about taking such a position? What makes this place of authority so impacting?

Encouragement from the COURAGEOUS

"…There are many earnest followers of Jesus from whom the meaning of this word [Abide in me], with the blessed experience it promises, is very much hidden. While trusting in the Saviour for pardon and for help, and seeking to some extent to obey Him, they have hardly realized to what closeness of union, to what intimacy of fellowship, to what wondrous oneness of life and interest, He invited them when He said, 'Abide in me.'"

—**Andrew Murray**[5]
[Words in brackets added for clarity.]

_____
_____
_____
_____
_____

He who heeds instruction and correction is [not only himself] in the way of life [but also] *is a way of life* for others. And he who neglects or refuses reproof [not only himself] goes astray [but also] causes to err and *is a path toward ruin* for others.
—**Proverbs 10:17 AMP**
[Italics added for emphasis.]

> "Countless Christians battle intimidation. Often those who are intimidated don't realize what they're fighting. As with most of Satan's devices, intimidation is *camouflaged* and subtle. We feel its effects—depression, confusion, lack of faith—without knowing its root. In frustration most of us deal with the aftermath, or *fruit*, of intimidation rather than with the *root* of intimidation itself. Therefore, we may experience temporary relief, but our struggles do not end."
> —**John Bevere** (adapted from pages 8, 9)

9. A spirit of fear or intimidation is a potent, paralyzing foe to face, but it can be conquered by the power of God living in you. Ask the Lord to open your spiritual eyes to see and understand how you are being held hostage by fear.

   a. What *types of fear* are you presently fighting against?
   _____
   _____
   _____

   b. What *symptoms* are you dealing with as a result?
   _____
   _____
   _____

   c. Have any gifts in your life become dormant because of this? If yes, which ones?
   _____
   _____
   _____

> "Be angry, and do not sin": do not let the sun go down on your wrath, nor *give **place*** to the devil.
> —**Ephesians 4:26-27**
> [Boldness and italics added for emphasis.]

PLACE

The original Greek word for *place* used in Ephesians 4:27 is *topos*. It generally refers to "a room, region, or location."⁶ In this verse, the word *place* also conveys the meaning of "opportunity, power, and occasion for acting."⁷ So when Paul says, "nor give place to the devil," in essence he is saying, "*Don't rent the devil a room in your soul* (your mind, will and emotions)—*don't give him occasion or opportunity to produce his rotten fruit in your life.*"

10. Satan often knocks at the door of our soul seeking an *opportunity* to gain entrance. He doesn't come with horns on his head and a pitch fork in his hand—he comes disguised as a steady flow of ungodly thoughts. Name some of the ways you've given Satan place in your life.

_____

_____

_____

_____

_____

_____

_____

> Don't *give place* to this venomous visitor. Learn to recognize and resist his thoughts quickly. **Check out** what 2 Corinthians 10:4-5 has to say about ordering your thoughts.

11. King David's sins of adultery, deception and murder carried crucial consequences for him, his family and the nation of Israel. As a parent, business owner, manager or Christian leader, your decisions and actions also have far-reaching effects on those under your authority.

   a. Have you ever done something wrong and then seen the same or similar behavior show up in your children or those under your care? Explain the situation.

   _____

   _____

   _____

   _____

   b. Is there any sin you need to repent of *right now*? Take some time to examine your heart; allow the Holy Spirit to shine the light of truth inside your soul. **Write out a prayer** asking God to forgive you and wash you clean of anything He reveals.

   _____

   _____

   _____

   _____

> "Just as he did with Adam in the Garden of Eden, Satan now seeks to displace us in the spirit in order to regain the authority Jesus stripped from him. If Satan can steal or cause individuals to lay down their position of authority, then he once again has authority to operate."
> —**John Bevere** (page 15)

FAITH FACTOR

As a believer, you have a God-given place of authority and function in the body of Christ. By God's grace, you must *be familiar with it* and *function in it* or the enemy will take it from you and use it against you and others.

MAKE IT Real

FINDING YOUR PLACE

> "Every one of you is called to do something for God. Every one of you has been gifted by God. If you yield to a spirit of intimidation, the gift in your life will grow dormant."
> —**John Bevere**
> (adapted from session 1)

To help you begin to identify what your place and function is, take a few moments to gather some information about yourself. You may even want to get the input of a trusted friend.

What do I like to do—what things bring me overall enjoyment, peace and fulfillment?

_____
_____
_____
_____
_____
_____

What am I good at doing—what things do I seem to be naturally "wired" to do?

_____
_____
_____
_____
_____
_____

Keep in mind, your heavenly Father is not going to ask you to do something that He does not give you the *power* and *desire* to do. As you work out your salvation in the reverent fear of the Lord, "…it is God Who is all the while effectually at work in you [energizing and creating in you the **power** and **desire**], both to will and to work for His good pleasure and satisfaction and delight" (Philippians 2:13 AMP).

If you already have a good idea of your place and function, jot it down here. As you do, ask the Lord to define and refine it more clearly for you.

_____
_____
_____
_____
_____
_____
_____
_____
_____
_____
_____
_____

"Please, Be Seated and *Stay* Seated."

> *And He raised us up together with Him and made us sit down together* ***[giving us joint seating with Him]*** *in the heavenly sphere [by virtue of our being] in Christ Jesus (the Messiah, the Anointed One).*
> **—Ephesians 2:6 AMP**
> [Boldness added for emphasis.]

Whether it's in a stadium watching your favorite sport, a night at the symphony, or watching your child perform in a special program, one thing is for sure—you want the best seat you can get. You want to be as close to the action as possible and able to see everything that's going on. Well, when it comes to your relationship with God, you have the best seat in the house!

There is no better place to be than next to the Creator of the universe, the Bright and Morning Star, the Son of the Living God—Jesus Christ! God has provided permanent reserved seating for you, as a believer, in Him in the heavenly realms. Consequently, **everything** that Jesus has is made available to you. Meditate for a moment on these powerful passages.

> He [*the Spirit of Truth*] will honor and glorify Me [*Jesus*], because He will take of (receive, draw upon) what is Mine and will reveal (declare, disclose, transmit) it to you. Everything that the Father has is Mine. That is what I meant when I said that He [the Spirit] will take the things that are Mine and will reveal (declare, disclose, transmit) it to you.
> —**John 16:14-15 AMP**
> [Words in italics added for clarity.]

> How we praise God, the Father of our Lord Jesus Christ, who has blessed us with **every** spiritual blessing in the heavenly realms because we belong to Christ.
> —**Ephesians 1:3 NLT**
> [Boldness added for emphasis.]

As a Christian, you are *in Christ*, and **everything** that Christ has is available to you—all authority, power, wisdom, direction, peace, love, joy and everything else you need; it's yours for the asking. As Jesus declares in John 15:7, "If you live in Me [abide vitally united to Me] and My words remain in you and continue to live in your hearts, ask whatever you will, and it shall be done for you" (AMP).

Kenneth E. Hagin ministered for nearly 70 years after God miraculously healed him of a deformed heart and an incurable blood disease at the age of 17. He is widely respected for his teachings concerning the faith and authority of believers. **Read** this insightful excerpt from his book, *The Believer's Authority*, and ask the Holy Spirit to reveal truth to you about being seated in Christ.

> "When Christ ascended, He transferred His authority to the church. He is the Head of the church, and believers make up the body. Christ's authority has to be perpetuated through His body, which is on the earth. …Christ is seated at the right hand of the Father—the place of authority—and we're seated with Him. If you know anything about history, you know that to sit at the right hand of the king or pope means authority. We died with Christ, and we were raised with Him. This is not something God is going to do in

the future; *He already has done it!*

…The act of God that raised Christ from the dead also raised His body. In the mind of God, when Jesus was raised from the dead, we were raised from the dead! Further into the second chapter we read, 'Even when we were dead in sins, [He] hath quickened us together with Christ, …And hath raised us up together, and made us sit together in heavenly places in Christ Jesus' (Ephesians 2:5-6 KJV). This passage deals with the conferring of this authority.

Notice that the Head (Christ) and the body (the church) were raised together. Furthermore, this authority was conferred not only upon the head, but also upon the body, because the head and the body are one. …When we realize that the authority that belongs to Christ also belongs to individual members of the body of Christ and is available to us, our lives will be revolutionized!"

—**Kenneth E. Hagin**[8]

Slowly **read** the excerpt again.

What insights is the Holy Spirit showing you about the power, authority and position of Jesus?

_____
_____
_____
_____
_____

What insights is He showing you about *your* power, authority and position *in Him*?

_____
_____
_____
_____
_____
_____
_____
_____

SEATED
To be placed on a seat and caused to sit down; to be placed in a post of authority, in office or a place of distinction; to settle, fix or set firm in a particular place.
—adapted from the *American Dictionary of the English Language*, **Noah Webster 1828**

> Since, then, you have been raised with Christ, set your hearts on things above, where Christ is seated at the right hand of God (NIV). And *set your minds* and *keep them set* on what is above (the higher things), not on the things that are on the earth. For [as far as this world is concerned] you have died, and your [new, real] life is hidden with Christ in God" (AMP).
> —**Colossians 3:1-3**
> [Italics added for emphasis.]

In order to be alive in Christ and remain seated in Him, we must *die to the desires of our flesh*. This is what it means to be *crucified with Christ*. **Read** the following verses, and in your own words **write** what it means to be crucified with Christ and why it is important.

- Romans 6:2,6,11
- Galatians 2:20; 5:24
- 1 Peter 2:24
- 2 Corinthians 4:11
- 2 Timothy 2:11

Your Place of Authority

How do we crucify our flesh and die to its desires? We learn to starve it. In other words, we ask God daily for His grace (power) to not give in to what *we want*, what *we think* and how *we feel*. Instead, we feed our spirit and follow after the promptings of the Holy Spirit (see Romans 6:12-13; Galatians 5:16). **Read** the following verses and ask the Lord to show you what it means to renew your mind. **Write** what He reveals.

- Psalm 51:10-12
- Romans 12:2
- Colossians 3:9-10
- Isaiah 40:31
- Ephesians 4:22-24

For Further Study

JESUS TALKS ABOUT BEING SEATED
Matthew 22:43-45
Matthew 26:64
Mark 16:19
Luke 22:67-69

THE APOSTLES TALK ABOUT JESUS BEING SEATED
Acts 2:32-35; 5:30-31
Philippians 2:9-11
Hebrews 1:13
1 Peter 3:21-22

Pen Your Progress

> "If people only knew where they are in Christ, they wouldn't come under intimidation."
> —**John Bevere** (adapted from session 1)

As you come to the end of this week's lesson, what is the most eye-opening truth the Holy Spirit is revealing to you? What Scripture(s) really hit home? How have your understanding of authority and your relationship with Christ been challenged? Write down any special things the Lord has shown you.

---

1. Charles Capps, *Authority in Three Worlds* (Tulsa, OK: Harrison House, Inc. 1980, 1982) pp. 217, 218. 2. Adapted from *Vine's Complete Expository Dictionary of Old and New Testament Words*, W. E. Vine (Nashville, TN: Thomas Nelson, Inc. 1996) p. 45. 3. Dennis R. Petersen, *Unlocking the Mysteries of Creation* (El Dorado, CA: Creation Resource Publication, 2002) p. 195. 4. See note 1. 5. Andrew Murray, *Abide in Christ* (New Kensington, PA: Whitaker House, 1979) p. 5. 6. See note 2, pp. 472, 473. 7. Thayer's Greek-English Lexicon of the New Testament, Joseph H. Thayer (Grand Rapids, MI: Baker Book House Company, 1977) p. 628. 8. Kenneth E. Hagin, *The Believer's Authority* (Tulsa, OK: Rhema Bible Church, 1986) pp. 11, 14-15.

Freedom Notes

"A Christian will backslide when he does not function in his gift or calling, just as a muscle atrophies with lack of use. You show me an idle Christian, and I will show you somebody who is headed for a fall."

—John Bevere
(adapted from session 2, page 35)

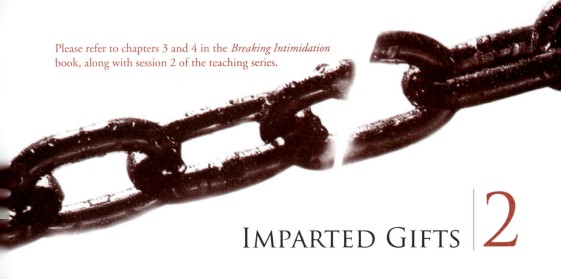

Please refer to chapters 3 and 4 in the *Breaking Intimidation* book, along with session 2 of the teaching series.

IMPARTED GIFTS | 2

> No one who is born of God will continue to sin, because *God's seed remains in him*; he cannot go on sinning, because he has been born of God.
> —**1 John 3:9 NIV**
> [Boldness and italics added for emphasis.]

Encouragement from the COURAGEOUS

"God gives us various *gifts* to use, but He gives us the *fruit* of the Spirit to develop. When the Holy Spirit lives inside us, we have everything He has. His fruit is in us. The **seed** has been planted. In order to use the gifts in the most powerful way that God desires, we must allow the seed of the fruit to grow up and mature in us by cultivating it. We can cultivate all the fruit by focusing on *love*, the first in the list of the nine fruits, and self-control, the last in the list. Love and self-control are like bookends that hold the rest in place. All of the fruit issue from love and actually are a form of love, but they are kept in place by self-control."

—**Joyce Meyer**[1]
[Boldness and italics added for emphasis.]

1. The *fruit* of the Spirit and the *gifts* of the Spirit—God wants you to have both. While the evidence of Christ's character is reflected in His fruit operating in your life, the evidence of His supernatural power is visible in the function of His gifts.

   a. What are the *nine* character traits, or fruit, of God's Spirit found in Galatians 5:22-23?

   _____
   _____
   _____
   _____

b. What are the *nine* gifts of God's Spirit found in 1 Corinthians 12:8-10?

c. What is the major difference between the *fruit* of the Spirit and *gifts* of the Spirit—that is, where do they come from and how do we get them?

2. Love is the greatest fruit of all, for out of it comes all the others. When we choose to *put on* love, we are pursuing the character of God because God **is** love (see 1 John 4:16). First Corinthians 14:1 says to *"pursue* love, and *desire* spiritual gifts…"

   a. What is the difference between *pursuing* and *desiring* something?

   b. **Write out** and **hide in your heart** these two related Scriptures:

   1 TIMOTHY 6:11 – PURSUE RIGHTEOUSNESS

   2 TIMOTHY 2:22 – FLEE YOUTHFUL LUSTS

Also **Check out** Psalm 34:14 and 1 Peter 4:11

> For I want you to understand what really matters, so that you may
> live pure and blameless lives until the day of Christ's return.
> May you always be filled with the *fruit* of your salvation—
> the righteous **character** produced in your life by Jesus Christ—
> for this will bring much glory and praise to God.
> —**Philippians 1:10-11 NLT vs.2**
> [Boldness and italics added for emphasis.]

CHARACTER

The word *character* is from a verb meaning "to scrape, cut, or engrave." With regard to people, character refers to "the peculiar qualities, *impressed* by nature or habit on a person, which distinguish him from others." When we develop Christ-like character, the unique qualities of His nature are *cut, impressed* or *engraved* into our character by the power of the Holy Spirit working in us.

—adapted from the *American Dictionary of the English Language*, **Noah Webster 1828**

3. Without question, *character counts*. Timothy had proven, godly character—the solid foundation upon which God's power can effectively be displayed and discharged.

   a. As a believer, what is the *correct* and *incorrect* way to measure your level of spiritual maturity?

   b. What is one thing you should never look at to gauge God's approval? Why is this dangerous?

4. It is so vital to have the proper balance in our spiritual walk. Without balance, we will falter and eventually fall. What *two extremes* must you guard against that will throw your life out of balance? Which of these do you have to guard against more?

_____
_____
_____
_____
_____

Encouragement from the COURAGEOUS

"God is forever on a quest. Ever thought about that? His pursuit is a subject woven through the fabric of the New Testament. The pattern He follows is set forth in Romans 8:29, where He promises to *conform* us to His Son's image. Another promise is stated in Philippians 1:6, where we're told He began His work in us and He isn't about to stop. Elsewhere He even calls us His 'workmanship' (Ephesians 2:10). He is hammering, filing, chiseling, and shaping us! Peter's second letter goes so far as to list some of the things included in this quest—diligence, faith, moral excellence, knowledge, self-control, perseverance, godliness, kindness, and *love* (2 Peter 1:5-7). In a word… **character**."

—**Charles R. Swindoll**[2]

[Boldness and italics added for emphasis.]

5. Desiring, understanding and flowing in the gifts of the Holy Spirit is *indispensable*, next to pursuing godly character. We need God's spiritual gifts in order to establish His church and effectively wage war in the realm of the spirit.

Meditate on the message of the following verses:

…But each man has his own **gift** from God; one has this gift, another has that.
—**1 Corinthians 7:7 NIV**

…Christ has given each of us *special abilities*—whatever he wants us to have out of his rich storehouse of *gifts*. The psalmist tells about this, for he says that when Christ returned triumphantly to heaven after his resurrection and victory over Satan, he gave generous **gifts** to men.
—**Ephesians 4:7-8 TLB**

As each one has received a **gift**, minister it to one another, as good stewards of the manifold grace of God.
—**1 Peter 4:10**

[Boldness and italics added for emphasis.]

What *three* principles about gifts can you identify in these verses?

_____
_____
_____
_____
_____

> "The church is the body of Christ. Just as our physical bodies contain many parts that differ in function and ability, even so the members of the body of Christ function in different callings and gifts. God determines their purpose and function. Each is important, and none is independent from the others."
> —**John Bevere** (pages 31, 32)

FOR QUESTIONS 6 AND 7, **READ** ROMANS 12:3-13, 1 CORINTHIANS 12 AND EPHESIANS 4:1-16.

GIFT

The word *gift* used in 1 Peter 4:10, 1 Corinthians 7:7, 1 Timothy 4:14, 2 Timothy 1:6 and Romans 11:29, 12:6 is from the Greek word *charisma*. "In essence, a *gift* is God's bestowed ability on an individual which empowers him or her to bear eternal fruit, which they could not otherwise bear on their own."³

6. The apostle Paul had a lot to say about the body of Christ and its diverse gifts and functions. Every believer makes up a part of the body, and *every* believer is supernaturally gifted to do something to strengthen and advance its outreach.

   a. Why did Jesus give us gifts, and why is it good that not all of us have the *same* gifts?

   Check out Ephesians 4:12-13 and 1 Corinthians 12:7, 14-19

   _____
   _____
   _____

   b. **Read** Romans 12:6-8, 1 Corinthians 12:27-28 and Ephesians 4:11. What does the *variety of gifts* among believers indicate and communicate to you?

   _____
   _____
   _____

IMPARTED GIFTS

c. Do you know what spiritual gift(s) God has given you? If so, what are they? If not, ask the Lord to reveal them.

> ...God has arranged the parts in the body, every one of them, just as *he* wanted them to be.
> **—1 Corinthians 12:18 NIV**
> [Italics added for emphasis.]

7. Just as our head houses our brain and functions as the command center for our physical body, Christ is the Head of the church, His body, and He works to bring direction to each of us through the voice of His Spirit living in us.

   a. In 1 Corinthians 12:4-6, 11-13 and Ephesians 4:4-6 there is *one* common thread of thought that runs throughout. What is it and why do you think it is significant?

   b. **Read** 1 Corinthians 12:14-24. Describe what your *attitude* should (and shouldn't) be toward the other parts of the body—your fellow brothers and sisters in Christ.

   c. Does your attitude need a "tuneup"? What do you need to repent of and ask God to change in you?

> A new command I give you: *Love one another.* As I have loved you, so you must love one another. By this all men will know that you are my disciples, if you love one another.
> —**John 13:34-35 NIV**
> [Italics added for emphasis.]

8. Like mortar binds the bricks of a building together, something powerful *binds believers together*. For the answer, **write out** and **hide in your heart** the following verses:

   COLOSSIANS 3:14

   Also **Check out** Ephesians 4:16

   _____
   _____
   _____
   _____

   1 CORINTHIANS 13:1-3, 13

   _____
   _____
   _____
   _____

> "While studying the lives of great men and women of God, I found that those who fell had become *idle* or *negligent* in their call. Perhaps they were still ministering, but it was under the natural momentum achieved by their previous years of ministry. They began to use God's gift for their own benefit, not to protect and serve others."
> —**John Bevere** (page 35)

CHECK OUT THE STORY OF DAVID AND BATHSHEBA IN 2 SAMUEL 11 AND 12:1-24.

9. King David was a dedicated, merciful man after God's heart. Yet, somewhere along the way he made some unwise decisions that led him into trouble. He *neglected* the gift and calling on his life and ended up coveting, stealing and committing adultery and murder.

   a. What did David do (or fail to do) that weakened him spiritually and made him vulnerable to temptation?

   _____
   _____

b. How did his actions affect him and his children?

c. What does this example speak to you personally?

> Do not *neglect* your gift, which was given you through a prophetic message when the body of elders laid their hands on you. Be diligent in these matters; give yourself wholly to them…
> —**1 Timothy 4:14-15 NIV**
> [Italics added for emphasis.]

10. To become idle or *neglect* your spiritual gifts means you *ignore, avoid, dismiss, despise* or *undervalue* the special abilities. A person who neglects the gift of God in his life tends to be a *peacekeeper* instead of a *peacemaker*. Explain the difference between the two. Which one are you more like?

Encouragement from the COURAGEOUS

"If you don't exercise your muscles, they weaken and atrophy. In the same way, if you don't utilize the abilities and skills God has given you, you will lose them. Jesus taught the parable of the talents to emphasize this truth. Referring to the servant who failed to use his one talent, the master said, 'Take the talent from him and give it to the one who has the ten talents.' Fail to use what you've been given and you'll lose it. Use the ability you've got and God will increase it."
—**Rick Warren**[4]

IMPARTED GIFTS 25

11. God desires and requires us to actively invest our gifts—our abilities, skills, talents and power—in the lives of others. **Read** the story of the master and the three servants in Matthew 25:14-30.

    a. How did the master determine how many talents to give each man? What did he want them to do with the talents?

    b. What godly character trait(s) did the servants with five talents and two talents display?

    c. What *un*godly character trait(s) kept the servant with one talent from using it?

    d. What is the Lord speaking to you personally about this story?

> "Nothing in the realm of the spirit is accomplished without this *charisma*, or supernatural ability of God. We should not preach, sing, prophesy, lead or even serve without it. There is no life produced without this grace. Lifeless religion is born out of man's attempt to serve God his own way, in his own ability. When we minister to others without the gifting of God, we labor in vain."
> —**John Bevere** (page 32)

> Unless the Lord builds the house, its builders labor in vain…
> —**Psalm 127:1 NIV**

12. Jesus said, "...My food (nourishment) is to do the will (pleasure) of Him Who sent Me and to accomplish and completely finish His work" (John 4:34 AMP). In the same way, a large part of our spiritual nourishment comes from being good stewards of God's gifts and doing His will.

Also **Check out** Matthew 25:21,23

a. What does it mean to be a *steward* of God's gift, and what's the reward of *good* stewardship?

___

b. If you draw back from using your gifts to do God's will, what will happen to *you*?

___

c. If you don't operate in the gifts God has given you, what will happen to *others* in the body of Christ?

___

> "What do you call a human being with only 20 percent of their body functioning? An **invalid**. That's what you call a church where only 20 percent of the people are operating in their gifts to benefit the kingdom. In the majority of our churches in America, 20 percent of the people are doing 80 percent of the work. But that is not the way God designed it. The reason our churches are not exploding is because we're not all operating in our gifts."
> —**John Bevere** (adapted from session 2)

FAITH FACTOR
Every believer has been given a special *gift* by God to use to bless and build up others in the body of Christ. As we pursue intimacy with the Father and the development of His character, we must also *stir up* the divine ability (gifts) He has placed in us and use them to serve others and bring Him glory.

IMPARTED GIFTS | 27

THE HONOR ROLL

Be devoted to one another in brotherly love. **Honor** one another above yourselves.
—**Romans 12:10 NIV**
[Boldness added for emphasis.]

Do you like to be appreciated for the work you do? Sure you do—we *all* do. There are people all around you—in the church and outside the church—whose souls are starved for some genuine appreciation. How can you give them what they need? One word says it all—*honor*.

Romans 12:10 says that we are to honor one another above ourselves. To *honor* means "to value, esteem, respect, treat favorably, and to have high regard for." A little praise can go a long way to promote healing and unity in your relationships and strengthen the overall success of others.

First Corinthians 12:24 says that God gives *greater honor* to the parts of the body that seem weaker or less important. They make *The Honor Roll*—God's Honor Roll!

Think for a moment…People who clean, straighten, build and repair things often go unnoticed and unthanked. This is also true of many who work with children. Although their job is not glamorous, it is still *extremely* important to the overall success of the church.

What parts of the **body of Christ** in your church family seem weaker or less important? What specific faces and names are coming to mind right now?

_____
_____
_____
_____
_____

How about your **fellow co-workers**? Who do you feel, in your heart, would greatly benefit from receiving honor? The person you want to honor the least may be the one who needs it the most.

_____
_____
_____
_____
_____

Get quiet and ask the Lord to show you *whom* He wants to honor and *how* you can honor them. He knows everybody and what will bless them best. Remember, what you do doesn't necessarily have to be big or expensive; it just has to be from the heart.

Here are some practical ideas to spark your imagination:

IDEA STARTERS
- Send them a special thank you card expressing your appreciation and include a gift certificate to a favorite restaurant or store.
- Verbally express your appreciation for all they do (be specific) and invite them to lunch or dinner at your house or a nice restaurant.
- Buy or bake their favorite kind of cake; include a special message of thanks on it and share it with some other church members or co-workers.
- Get an oversized card and pass it around for people to sign and express their appreciation.
- Send a bouquet of flowers or a special plant with a card expressing thanks.

Placing people on *The Honor Roll* is not a one-time event—it's a way of life. Allow the Lord to take this activity and use it to make you a flowing fountain of blessings to the people He's placed around you. Your life will be enriched immeasurably!

> So then, as occasion and opportunity open up to us, let us do good [morally] to all people [not only being useful or profitable to them, but also doing what is for their spiritual good and advantage]. Be mindful to be a blessing, especially to those of the household of faith [those who belong to God's family with you, the believers].
> **—Galatians 6:10 AMP**
> [Boldness and italics added for emphasis.]

MY PLAN TO HONOR _____ IS...

_____
_____
_____
_____
_____
_____

THE *ONE* THING

> …everything else is worthless when compared with the priceless gain of **knowing Christ Jesus my Lord**. I have put aside all else, counting it worth less than nothing, in order that I can have Christ, and become one with him…
> —**Philippians 3:8-9 TLB**
> [Boldness added for emphasis.]

There are countless things that cry out for your attention—some good and some bad. It may be your job, spouse, children, entertainment, friends, extended family, worldly pleasures, ministry commitments, and the list goes on. The fact is that you have opportunities every day to chase after any number of these things. Yet amidst all of them, there is only *one thing* that truly matters most…there is only *one thing* that is truly fulfilling…there is only one thing that truly deserves first place. That one thing is *intimacy with the Lord*.

The apostle **Paul** knew about the power of passionately pursuing Christ. He counted everything else as *worthless* in comparison to knowing the Lord intimately (see Philippians 3:8-9). King **David** also knew the priceless privilege of being in God's presence. He passionately proclaimed, "*One thing* have I asked of the Lord, that will I seek, inquire for, and [insistently] require: that I may dwell in the house of the Lord [in His presence] all the days of my life…" (Psalm 27:4 AMP).

Jesus Himself shined a spotlight on the importance of spending time with Him. When Martha became frustrated over her sister Mary's lack of assistance during one of His visits, He told her, "…Martha, dear Martha, you're fussing far too much and getting yourself worked up over nothing. **One thing** only is essential, and Mary has chosen it—it's the main course, and won't be taken from her" (Luke 10:41-42 The Message).

Ponder These Promises

> "When you come looking for me, you'll find me. Yes, when you get serious about finding me and want it *more than anything else*, I'll make sure you won't be disappointed." God's Decree.
> —**Jeremiah 29:13 The Message**

You have said, *Seek My face* [inquire for and require My presence as your vital need]. My heart says to You, Your face (Your presence),

Lord, will I seek, inquire for, and require [of necessity
and on the authority of Your Word].
—**Psalm 27:8 AMP**

But seek (aim at and strive after) *first of all* His kingdom and
His righteousness (His way of doing and being right), and then
all these things taken together will be given you besides.
—**Matthew 6:33 AMP**
[Italics added for emphasis.]

Author, songwriter and mother of four, Frances J. Roberts, wrote a best-selling book titled *Come Away My Beloved*. Carefully **read** this insightful excerpt from her book and listen for the Lord's tender call to you:

"I know thy need, and I am concerned for thee: for thy peace, for thy health, for thy strength. I cannot use a tired body, and ye need to take time to renew thine energies, both spiritual and physical. I am the God of Battle, but I am also the One who said: They that wait upon the Lord shall renew their strength. And Jesus said, Come ye apart and rest a little while.

…As ye give Me My rightful place and do not allow others to intrude, ye shall be at peace with Me. Be very serious in this. I am not speaking to thee lightly. I was never more in earnest in any message that I have brought to you. Do not fail Me. I have brought you this message at various times in the past. It was never more urgent than now.

For man is experiencing a new awakening, and he is searching for My Truth more than ever, and I must speak through My prophets; and if they be not separated unto Me, how can I instruct them? Yea, I shall nourish thee by the brook as I nourished Elijah; and I shall speak to thee out of the bush as I spoke to Moses, and reveal My glory on the hillside as I did to the shepherds.

COME AWAY, MY BELOVED, and be as the doe upon the mountains; yea, we shall go down together to the gardens."
—**Frances J. Roberts**[5]

What is the Lord speaking to you right now about spending intimate time with Him?

_____
_____
_____
_____

IMPARTED GIFTS

What things in your life are competing for first place and crowding out your intimate time with the Lord? Write them down and surrender them to Him.

_____
_____
_____
_____
_____
_____

Get quiet and ask the Holy Spirit to show you specifically what you need to adjust or rearrange in your routine to give the Lord His place of preeminence in your day.

_____
_____
_____
_____
_____
_____

God has stated many times, in many ways throughout Scripture, the powerful importance of putting Him first and spending time with Him. He loves you *intensely* and deeply desires to be welcomed into every area of your life. James 4:5 says, "…The Spirit Whom He has caused to dwell in us *yearns* over us and He yearns for the Spirit [to be welcome] with a jealous love!" (AMP).

Will you put the welcome mat out for the Creator of the universe and the Lover of your soul? He's standing at the door of your heart knocking. *Please*, let Him in—not just once on Sunday, but every day in every way. He will cultivate His character in you—He will grant you the gifts of His Spirit and show you how, when and where to use them. Your life will never be the same!

PRAYER OF DEDICATION

Father, forgive me for not seeking after You more. I know in my heart You are the answer to every problem I will ever face and the provision for every need I will ever have. I desperately need You in my life; give me a desire for You like You have for me. Help me put You first every day. Give me a specific plan on how, when and where I can spend special time alone with You. You know all my responsibilities and commitments; show me anything I need to let go of and give me the grace to follow through. Thank You for this lesson on the gifts of the Spirit. Help me to see clearly what gifts You have given me and how to use them. I love You, Lord, and I thank You for loving and accepting me unconditionally. In Jesus' name, Amen.

RECOMMENDED READING
Experiencing God by Henry T. Blackaby & Claude V. King, Broadman & Holman Publishers, Nashville, TN 1994.
The Secret's of the Secret Place by Bob Sorge, Oasis House, Lee's Summit, MO 2005.

WHO AM I?
Find and define *your* place in the body of Christ.

Explore the landscape of your life and the inner core of who you are! Get alone with the Lord and ask yourself...

What are my *spiritual gifts*? After reading Romans 12, 1 Corinthians 12 and Ephesians 4, what divine abilities has God entrusted to me? In what ways is He using me in my local church?

What's my *heartbeat*? In the deepest part of who I am, what are my hopes, dreams and passions? If I could do anything at all and age, education, money, health, etc. were *not* an obstacle, what would I do?

What are my *abilities*? What do I enjoy and am naturally good at—sports, music, research, public speaking, helping others? What have my trusted friends and family members said I am good at?

What's my *personality*? Am I laid back or do I like a lot of attention? Do I like to be in charge? Am I organized and good with details? Do I like to use my hands, mouth or mind most?

How has my *relationship with God* been? What times have I felt closest to the heart of God? If I have served in ministry, what were my most *enjoyable* and *fruitful* positions of serving?

What are my *experiences*? What have I learned from life while growing up at home, in school and in church? What jobs did I enjoy and was really good at? What painful troubles have I learned from?

Remember, there are no *wrong* answers. Answer honestly and allow the Lord to unveil who you really are and where your place is in His body. Write your answers down in a journal or notebook.

IMPARTED GIFTS

> "God wants you liberated to do and be whatever He asks of you. When you are intimidated, there is *no joy*. And without joy there is *no strength*. Where there is fear, there is *no peace*. But as you break out of what has held you back, you'll find joy and peace in abundance!"
> **—John Bevere** (page 29)

The return of our Lord is close at hand. Therefore, it is crucial that you passionately pursue His presence, know your gifts, and give yourself to them. Every member of His body is a minister—not just your pastor. God is counting on *you* to use what He's given you to edify others and multiply the church's effectiveness. Do you know what your gift is? Are you operating in it? Write what the Holy Spirit is revealing to you through this lesson, as well as anything He's asking you to do in response.

1. Joyce Meyer, *Secrets to Exceptional Living* (Tulsa, OK: Harrison House, Inc., 2002) p. 14. 2. Charles R. Swindoll, *The Quest for Character* (Portland, OR: Multnomah Press, 1987) p.14. 3. John Bevere, *Breaking Intimidation Session 2*, recorded June 22, 2008. 4. Rick Warren, *The Purpose Driven Life* (Grand Rapids, MI: Zondervan, 2002) p. 255. 5. Frances J. Roberts, *Come Away My Beloved* (Ojai, CA: King's Farspan, Inc., 1973) pp. 145, 146.

Imparted Gifts

Freedom Notes

"Any time we open ourselves up to fear, we fall prey to his deceptions and intimidations. Yet, if we submit our hearts to God and stand in faith, we can resist those first fearful thoughts. As we yield to God we can master our reactions to fear and the enemy will soon flee."

—**Francis Frangipane**[1]

Please refer to chapter 5 in the *Breaking Intimidation* book, along with session 3 of the teaching series.

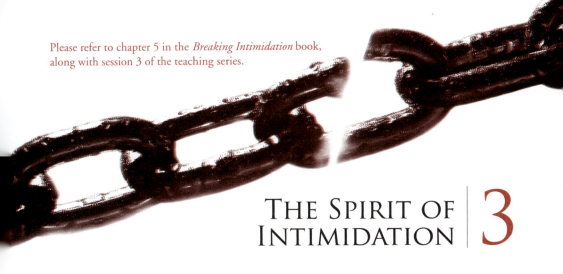

THE SPIRIT OF INTIMIDATION | 3

> "Intimidated believers lose their authority in the spirit by default [avoiding or evading the situation]; consequently, their gift—God's ability in them—lies asleep and inactive. Though it is present, it is not in operation. …If intimidation is not dealt with immediately, it will cause you to do things you never would do if you were not under its influence."
> —**John Bevere** (pages 45, 48)
> [Words in brackets added for clarity.]

> Therefore I remind you to stir up the gift of God which is in you through the laying on of my hands. For [because] God has not given us a spirit of fear [timidity], but of power and of love and of a sound mind.
> —**2 Timothy 1:6-7**
> [Words in brackets added for clarity.]

1. Even though we are seated in heavenly places with Christ—*far above* all the enemy's power—and *all* authority has been given to us through Christ, we can still become captive to a spirit of intimidation.

    a. Have your gifts become *dormant*—have you surrendered your position of authority? Who or what in your life is being used by Satan to intimidate you? Ask God to show you.

    _____
    _____
    _____
    _____
    _____

b. What does it mean to *stir up* the gift of God in you?

2. In the minds of many Christians, there is a common misunderstanding concerning the gifts of God's Spirit *automatically* operating in our lives. What is it?

INTIMIDATE

Merriam-Webster's Collegiate Dictionary defines *intimidate* as: "to discourage, coerce, or suppress by (or as if by) threatening." *The Oxford English Dictionary* defines it as: "to render timid; to inspire with fear." It defines *intimidation* as "the action of intimidating or making afraid; the use of threats or violence to force or restrain from some action."[2]

3. Recognizing a spirit of intimidation and understanding how it works are major keys to victory.

   a. In what specific *ways*, or avenues, does a spirit of intimidation attack?

   b. What are the common *symptoms*, or fruit, that confirm a spirit of intimidation is operating in your life? How is your relationship with God usually affected?

c. Are you presently dealing with any of these symptoms? If so, which ones and how long have you been dealing with them?

d. What is a spirit of intimidation's ultimate goal in attacking you?

> "Once you've retreated into submission, either knowingly or *unknowingly*, you are a servant of the intimidator. You are no longer free to fulfill the will of God but are doomed to the desires of your intimidating captor. Consequently, the gift of God, His spiritual ability in you, is *inoperative*. Now your authority has been stripped from you in order to be used against both you and those in your sphere of influence."
> **—John Bevere** (page 46)

4. Many people who are under an attack of intimidation fail to recognize exactly what they are dealing with. As a result, they fight to get rid of the *fruit* of their problems—the inner feelings of dissatisfaction—but never get to the *root*.

   a. What are some of the ways in which people try to deal with the fruit of intimidation?

   b. What are the downfalls to just dealing with the fruit (symptoms)?

c. Since intimidation is a *spirit*, what is the *only* successful way it can be defeated?

___

> For we are not fighting against *people* made of flesh and blood, but against the evil rulers and authorities of the unseen world, against those mighty powers of darkness who rule this world, and against wicked *spirits* in the heavenly realms.
> —**Ephesians 6:12 NLT**
> [Italics added for emphasis.]

Encouragement from the COURAGEOUS

"We are locked in a battle. This is not a friendly, gentleman's discussion. It is a *life and death conflict* between the spiritual hosts of wickedness and those who claim the name of Christ."
—**Francis A. Schaeffer**[3]
[Italics added for emphasis.]

5. Jesus said, "No one can enter a strong man's house and plunder his goods, unless he first binds the strong man. And then he will plunder his house" (Mark 3:27). Who is the *strong man* and what do his *house* and his *goods* represent?

___

6. Elijah was a powerful prophet of God who moved in the miraculous. In one day of ministry, he built a huge altar, prepared a sacrifice, killed 850 prophets of Baal, and outran Ahab's chariot. Yet at the end of the day, he *gave place* to a spirit of intimidation that brought his ministry to a virtual standstill.

*Hint: **Check out** what Elijah did in 1 Kings 19:4-8*

a. In light of all the energy Elijah exerted that day, what things in the *natural* probably played a part in making him vulnerable to a spirit of intimidation released through Jezebel?

___

b. What does this speak to you personally?

c. God wanted Elijah to *confront* the source of the sin—Jezebel. Is there a certain situation in which God is asking *you* to stand against unrighteousness? If so, share it.

> "Jezebel was the motivating influence behind the wickedness that had crept into Israel. If the wrong influence of a leader is not confronted and put to a stop, then it is only a matter of time before the wickedness filters down to those under their charge."
> **—John Bevere** (page 51)

7. What happened in the realm of the spirit when Elijah didn't confront Jezebel and ran for his life? How did his actions affect the people and nation of Israel?

8. Like Elijah, have you ever been so overwhelmingly depressed that you wanted to die? If you have, describe the situation and share how God pulled you out of it. Looking back, can you now see what the enemy was trying to do? What good did God bring out of it?

> [What, what would have become of me] had I not believed that I would see the Lord's goodness in the land of the living! Wait and *hope for* and *expect the Lord*; be brave and of good courage and let your heart be stout and enduring. Yes, wait for and hope for and expect the Lord.
> **—Psalm 27:13-14 AMP**
> [Italics added for emphasis.]

9. As an instrument in the enemy's hands, Jezebel controlled her husband, Ahab, through intimidation and manipulation, and thereby held the authority of the kingdom.

   a. Have *you* ever been used by the enemy to intimidate and manipulate someone? If so, who was it and what happened?

   _____
   _____
   _____
   _____

   b. Get quiet and ask the Lord to show you *how* and *why* you ended up being used by the enemy. Write what He reveals.

   _____
   _____
   _____
   _____

   Take a moment to repent to God for being a part of the enemy's plan. Ask God to forgive you and wash you clean. Receive His forgiveness and move on.

COURAGE and ENCOURAGE

The word *courage* comes from an original root word meaning "heart." *Courage* is "bravery, boldness, valor, resolution; that quality of mind which enables men to encounter danger and difficulties with firmness, or without fear or depression of spirits." To *encourage* means "to give courage to; to give or increase confidence of success; to inspire with courage, spirit, or strength of mind; to embolden; to animate; to incite; to inspirit."
—adapted from the *American Dictionary of the English Language*, **Noah Webster 1828**

The Spirit of Intimidation

10. After Moses died, the mantle of leadership over Israel passed to his assistant Joshua. Imagine the overwhelming immensity of the task given to him. Undoubtedly, the enemy tried to intimidate him and keep him from the destiny God had planned, but God did not leave Joshua alone. **Read** the empowering message He delivered to him in Joshua 1:1-9.

   a. Three times God told Joshua to *be strong and courageous*. What does this signify about Joshua?

   _____
   _____
   _____
   _____

   b. On what grounds was Joshua not to fear?

   _____
   _____
   _____
   _____

   > **Check out** verses 5 and 9

   Also found in Exodus 33:14, Isaiah 43:2 and Matthew 28:20.

   c. **Write out** and **hide in your heart** Joshua 1:7-8, revealing the two major keys to remaining strong and courageous.

   JOSHUA 1:7-8

   _____
   _____
   _____
   _____
   _____
   _____
   _____
   _____
   _____

   > *Encouragement* from the **COURAGEOUS**
   >
   > "In any trial, in any bitter situation, *you are not alone*, you are not helpless, you are not a victim. You have a tree, a cross, shown to you by the Sovereign God of Calvary. Whatever the trial or temptation, it is not more than you can bear. It is bearable. It can be handled. You can know as Joseph knew, "You meant evil against me, but God meant it for good in order to bring about this present result, to preserve many people alive" (Genesis 50:20).
   > —Kay Arthur[4]

11. In the face of fearful and intimidating situations, God repeatedly commanded His people to be *strong* and *courageous*, or full of courage. God is the same yesterday, today and forever, and He is speaking the same thing to you today. Hear Him through the voice of His Word—**write out** and **hide in your heart** these related power principles:

JOSHUA 1:9

_____
_____
_____
_____
_____

ISAIAH 41:10,13

_____
_____
_____
_____
_____

> Be strong. Take courage. *Don't be intimidated.* Don't give them
> a second thought because God, your God, is striding ahead of you.
> He's right there with you. He won't let you down; he won't leave you.
> —**Deuteronomy 31:6 The Message**
> [Italics added for emphasis.]

FAITH FACTOR
When you *give place* to a spirit of intimidation, the gift of God in you will become dormant. Therefore, it is absolutely imperative that you learn how to recognize and resist a spirit of intimidation; you must deal with the root, not just the fruit.

The Spirit of Intimidation

MAKE IT Real

HE TOOK THE WORDS RIGHT OUT OF MY MOUTH!

"Demons ride on words. I have a very close friend in ministry who had a vision of a bunch of demons sitting on surf boards, and they were waiting for the wave. You know what the wave was? The wave was *what people spoke*, and the only way the demons could get momentum or get anything done was to ride the *waves of words*. That's why you want to watch what you are saying; you don't want to be cooperating with evil forces."

—**John Bevere**
(adapted from session 3)

What *words* and *phrases* commonly come out of your mouth? Are they words of faith or words of fear? When you speak fearful, negative words you attract the enemy, just like a magnet is attracted to metal. First Peter 5:8 says that Satan roams around like a hungry lion seeking someone to devour. Fearful, negative words send out a scent in the devil's direction—like ringing a dinner bell in his ears.

On the other hand, when you speak words of faith that are filled with Scripture, you draw God's attention and power into your life. In Jeremiah 1:12 God says, "…I am alert and active, watching over My word to perform it" (AMP). How does God perform His Word? He orchestrates His actions through His angels—His mighty ones who do His commandments, hearkening to the voice of His word (see Psalm 103:20 AMP). Indeed, God is *hungry* to fellowship with you and show Himself strong in your life (see 2 Chronicles 16:9).

The reality is that what you are *full* of is going to come out of your mouth. Jesus said in Luke 6:45 that out of the overflow of our hearts our mouths speak. Surely, He knew the power of words. Just before going to the Cross, He told His disciples, "I will no longer talk much with you, for the ruler of this world is coming, and he has nothing in Me" (John 14:30). When under unbelievable pressure, He knew it was best to keep His mouth closed and not give the enemy any ammunition to operate in His life.

> **Words** satisfy the mind as much as fruit does the stomach; *good talk* is as gratifying as a good harvest. **Words** *kill*, words give *life*; they're either poison or fruit—you choose.
> —**Proverbs 18:20-21 The Message**
> [Boldness and italics added for emphasis.]

Get quiet before the Lord and ask Him to bring to your mind any fearful phrases or words of worry that often flow from your lips.

___

Are you allowing the state of the economy to dictate the way you view and handle your finances? What phrases or words prove this?

___

Encouragement from the COURAGEOUS

"Spoken words program your spirit (heart) either to *success* or *defeat*. **Words are containers**. They carry *faith*, or *fear*, and they produce after their kind. 'So then faith cometh by hearing, and hearing by the word of God' (Romans 10:17 KJV). Faith comes more quickly when you hear yourself quoting, speaking, and saying the things God said. You will more readily receive God's Word into your spirit by hearing yourself say it than if you hear someone else say it."
—**Charles Capps**[5]
[Boldness and italics added for emphasis.]

RENEW YOUR *MIND* AND YOUR *MOUTH*!

From the previous questions, select a phrase you often say that needs to change. Using a Bible concordance, find *two* Scriptures that are positive alternatives to the fearful, negative phrases you've been speaking. Personalize the verses, commit them to memory and begin speaking them out loud over your life.

Scripture Reference

___

Scripture Reference

_____
_____
_____
_____
_____
_____

Sample faith-filled confessions: "The Lord is my Shepherd [to feed, guide, and shield me], I shall not lack" (Psalm 23:1 AMP). "I have been faithful to God, and He will supply all of my needs according to His riches in glory" (adapted from Philippians 4:19). "I am anointed to prosper on a level the church and the world are not familiar with, all for the glory of God!"

Fill your mind and mouth with the fire of God's Word and watch how the world around you explodes with His goodness!

PRAYER OF CLEANSING

Dear Father, please forgive me for speaking words of fear instead of words of faith. Help me discipline myself to get my mind and mouth in agreement with Your Word. "Set a guard over my mouth, O Lord; keep watch over the door of my lips" (Psalm 141:3 NIV). For "he who guards his lips guards his life, but he who speaks rashly will come to ruin" (Proverbs 13:3 NIV). Let my conversation always be full of grace—not negative, fearful phrases that attract the enemy (see Colossians 4:6). I love You, Lord, and I thank You for helping me make Your powerful, positive words a permanent part of my vocabulary. In Jesus' name, Amen.

GETTING TO THE *ROOT* OF THE PROBLEM

> But I, God, search the heart and examine the mind.
> I get to the heart of the human. I get to the ROOT of things.
> —**Jeremiah 17:10 The Message**

Think about *roots*. They are the most important part of a plant. They *lie under* the ground and are responsible for securing a plant in the earth. Roots stretch out and soak up water from the surrounding soil to keep the plant alive; they draw nutrients from the ground and make them usable for the plant to produce fruit. Without roots, a plant can't survive, much less produce fruit.

Amazingly, the function of roots in the natural paints a powerful portrait of what takes place in the realm of the spirit. Ungodly roots are the *underlying* source of our problems. While the roots of a plant anchor it in the earth, the roots of our ungodly thoughts, feelings and actions anchor our problems in the soil of our soul. Rotten roots produce rotten fruit. In order to get rid of the rotten fruit, we must get rid of the rotten roots.

ROOT

"That part of a plant which enters and fixes itself in the earth, and serves to support the plant in an erect position, while by means of its fibers it absorbs nutrients for the stem, branches and fruit."
—adapted from *American Dictionary of the English Language*, **Noah Webster 1828**

"The problem is that so many Christians don't deal with the *root*—they deal with the *fruit*. So many Christians are wondering, 'Why am I fighting so much depression? Why am I constantly fighting a lack of vision and hopelessness? I'm a believer. Why is it that I am having to work myself up to even have hope?' These are the symptoms of a spirit of intimidation."
—**John Bevere** (adapted from session 3)

A spirit of intimidation is the root cause of many problems. How can you know if you are dealing with a spirit of intimidation? Look and see what kind of fruit is manifesting in your life. The fruit are the *symptoms* that show up in your thoughts, feelings, actions and sometimes even your physical body.

Think about it. When you are sick, you go to the doctor. He asks you, "What kind of symptoms are you having?" If you are manifesting the symptoms of fever, headache, sore throat, joint pain and chills, there is a good chance you are dealing with the flu. The *symptoms* help identify the *source* of the problem and give direction to the doctor on the best method and medicine with which to treat you.

In Scripture, one of the names Jesus is referred to as is the *Great Physician*. The wonderful thing about His doctoring is that He isn't just practicing medicine—He has a proven cure! Get quiet before the Lord and pray as David did in Psalm 139:23-24, asking the Great Physician to search out and investigate the inner workings of your soul. Tell Him your symptoms and let Him prep you for a spiritual operation that will heal you from the inside out!

THE SPIRIT OF INTIMIDATION

> *Investigate* my life, O God, find out everything about me;
> *cross-examine* and test me, get a clear picture of what I'm about;
> see for yourself whether I've done anything wrong—
> then guide me on the road to eternal life.
> **—Psalm 139:23-24 The Message**
> [Italics added for emphasis.]

According to 1 Timothy 6:10, what is the *root of all evil* that you must keep weeded out of your life?

_____
_____
_____
_____

Read Hebrews 12:15 and identify the radical root that can grow quickly and choke out the life of a believer if he or she is not careful. What makes this root so dangerous?

_____
_____
_____
_____
_____

God *does* want roots in you, but He wants *righteous* roots that produce righteous fruit. These grow from the divine Seed of God planted in you the moment you repent of your sins and invite Christ into your heart (see 1 John 3:9). Regularly applying the *water of the Word* and soaking in the "Sonlight" of God's presence will yield a healthy harvest of righteousness in you!

Why is it so important that you not just hear the Word but also allow God to root it in you?

Check out these verses on the Parable of the Sower—Matthew 13:20-22

_____
_____
_____
_____
_____
_____

Write out these two passages, revealing what God wants rooted in you:

COLOSSIANS 2:6-7

_____
_____
_____
_____

EPHESIANS 3:17-19

_____
_____
_____
_____

> I, Jesus…**am the Root** (the Source) and the Offspring of David, the radiant and brilliant Morning Star.
> —**Revelation 22:16 AMP**
> [Boldness added for emphasis.]

Pen Your Progress

What is the Lord speaking to you through this week's lesson? Do you see the frustrating symptoms of your life in a different light? Take a few moments to reflect upon what the Holy Spirit is showing you. Write down any special things He reveals.

_____
_____
_____
_____
_____
_____

---

1. Quotes on *Spiritual Warfare* (www.dailychristianquote.com, retrieved 8/8/08). 2. John Bevere, *Breaking Intimidation* (Lake Mary, FL: Charisma House, 1995, 2006) pp. 45, 46. 3. See note 1. 4. Quotes on *Strength in Times of Adversity*, see note 1. 5. Charles Capps, *God's Creative Power Will Work for You* (Tulsa, OK: Harrison House, Inc. 1976) p. 7.

Freedom Notes

"Almighty God, who created us in Your image: Grant us grace fearlessly to contend against evil and to make no peace with oppression; and, that we may reverently use our freedom, help us to employ it in the maintenance of justice in our communities and among the nations, to the glory of Your holy name; through Jesus Christ our Lord, who lives and reigns with You and the Holy Spirit, one God, now and forever. Amen."

—William Wilberforce[1]

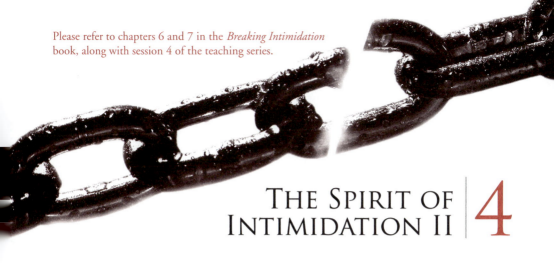

Please refer to chapters 6 and 7 in the *Breaking Intimidation* book, along with session 4 of the teaching series.

The Spirit of Intimidation II | 4

"Intimidation is *not* an attitude or a disposition. It is a *spirit*. Since intimidation is a spirit, it cannot be fought on the level of our intellect or will. Having a positive mental attitude will *not* overcome intimidation. Spiritual *resistance* requires spiritual *assistance*. It must be addressed in the realm of the spirit."
—**John Bevere** (adapted from pages 69, 70)

For God has not given us a *spirit* of fear,
but of power and of love and of a sound mind.
—**2 Timothy 1:7**
[Italics added for emphasis.]

1. If you *give place* to a spirit of intimidation, you come under its control and open a door for fear to enter your heart.

    a. Name some of the things you stand to lose when you allow fear to enter your heart.

    _____
    _____
    _____
    _____
    _____
    _____
    _____

SPIRIT

The word *spirit* used in 2 Timothy 1:7 is the Greek word *pneuma*. In this verse it specifically means "in opposition to the divine [Holy] Spirit; a spirit that comes from the devil [a demon]; the spirit that actuates [activates, motivates, sets in motion] the unholy multitude [unbelievers] and enslaves their lives in bondage."[2]
[Words in brackets added for clarity.]

b. What does a spirit of intimidation cause you to focus on?

c. **Write out** and **hide in your heart** Hebrews 12:2, revealing what you should focus on.

HEBREWS 12:2

2. A spirit of intimidation cannot operate wherever it wants; it can only operate through a person who will *yield* to it. To successfully stay free or break free from its grips, action must be taken.

   a. What happens when you *ignore* a spirit of intimidation?

Check out
1 Corinthians 12:8-10

   b. Since recognizing that the spirit you are fighting is so important, what spiritual gift should you ask God for?

   c. **Write out** and **hide in your heart** these passages, telling you *how* and *where* to live.

GALATIANS 5:16

THE SPIRIT OF INTIMIDATION II

ROMANS 8:5-6

_____
_____
_____
_____
_____

3. Are you working under or with someone who has an intimidating spirit? Who is it? How does the spirit manifest against you—how does it make you feel afraid, discouraged, paralyzed or controlled? How have you responded?

_____
_____
_____
_____
_____

> He sends forth His word and
> *heals* them and *rescues* them
> from the pit and destruction.
> —**Psalm 107:20 AMP**
> [Italics added for emphasis.]

4. During the years when Eli ruled as judge and high priest, the Bible says that "…the Word of the Lord was *rare* in those days; there was no widespread revelation" (1 Samuel 3:1).

   a. What does "the Word of the Lord was rare" mean, and *why* was this the case?

_____
_____
_____
_____

Encouragement from the COURAGEOUS

"…The soul can do without everything *except* the Word of God… there is no more cruel stroke of the wrath of God than when He sends a famine of hearing His words, just as there is no greater favour from Him than the sending forth of His word…"

—**Martin Luther**[3]
[Italics added for emphasis.]

b. What happens to God's people when His Word is rare?

Check out
Deuteronomy
8:3 and
Luke 4:4

c. How important is the Word of God to you *personally*? Is it rare or common in your life?

> …But now the Lord says: '…those who honor Me I will honor, and those who despise Me shall be lightly esteemed.'
> —**1 Samuel 2:30**

"An intimidated person honors what he *fears* more than he honors God. With or without realizing it, he *submits* to what intimidates him."
—**John Bevere** (session 4)

5. Like Eli, many parents are intimidated by their children—they feel *threatened* and *suppressed*, and some are even *paralyzed* by fear. As a result, they honor their children more than God and fail to give them the discipline they desperately need.

   a. Are you honoring your children, spouse, friends or someone else *more than* God? If so, whom?

   b. What is the fruit of a home where parents are intimidated by their children? Are you experiencing any of this fruit?

c. Get quiet and honestly ask the Lord, *Am I intimidated by my children?* If so, ask Him to show you why and what you need to do to break free from it.

6. Why did God seek to kill Moses when he was on his way back to Egypt? (See Exodus 4:24-26.) With whom was Moses intimidated? What does this example speak to you personally?

> If we [freely] *admit* that we have sinned and *confess* our sins, He is faithful and just (true to His own nature and promises) and will forgive our sins [dismiss our lawlessness] and [*continuously*] cleanse us from all unrighteousness [everything not in conformity to His will in purpose, thought, and action].
> **—1 John 1:9 AMP**
> [Italics added for emphasis.]

7. As cancer is to the human body, so unrestrained sin is to the human soul. God said He would judge Eli and his family "...because of the sin *he knew about*; his sons made themselves contemptible, and *he failed to restrain them*" (1 Samuel 3:13 NIV).

Encouragement from the COURAGEOUS

"There is one truth that runs through the whole Bible: *God will never compromise with sin.* ... Many Christians today are speaking and praying about 'revival.' They often overlook the fact that there is one barrier to revival that can never be bypassed. It is *sin*. Until sin is dealt with, true revival can never come. And **there is only one way to deal with sin:** 'He who covers his sins will not prosper, but whoever confesses and forsakes them will have mercy' (Proverbs 28:13)."
—**Derek Prince**[4]
[Boldness added for emphasis.]

a. As a true believer, what should your attitude be toward sin?

___

Check out
1 Corinthians 5:6 and Ecclesiastes 10:1

b. Why is it so important to deal with *known*, *willful* sin in your life and your family, even if it seems to be small and insignificant? What will happen if you don't deal with it?

___

c. When God places you in any position of authority, what does He expect you to do?

___

d. **Write out** and **hide in your heart** the related power principle in James 4:17:

JAMES 4:17

___

> A *little* leaven (a slight inclination to error, or a few false teachers) leavens the whole lump [it perverts the whole conception of faith or misleads the whole church].
> **—Galatians 5:9 AMP**
> [Italics added for emphasis.]

FASCINATING FACT
A LITTLE GOES A LONG WAY

Leaven is a type of *yeast*, which is generally a symbol of corruption or sin in both the Old and New Testament. The image being communicated in Galatians 5:9 is that just as a tiny amount of yeast is able to permeate and **ferment** a large amount of dough, a small amount of *known*, *deliberate* sin in a person or a group that is *tolerated* will eventually spread and infect the entire individual or group.

Interestingly, the word *fermentation* means "chemical decomposition of an organic substance (as in the souring of milk)."[5] In its most general sense, *fermentation* is "any spontaneous change which takes place in animal or vegetable substances, *after life has ceased*."[6] Tolerating sin in our lives is tolerating something that will eventually cause the decomposition, or decay, of our faith to the point of spiritual death.

> For more on leaven, **Check out** Exodus 12:15-20; Deuteronomy 16:1-4, 8; Matthew 16:5-12

8. Your pastor, who is a shepherd of God, is called to *feed* and *protect* the people under his care. A major part of this protection includes:

    a. Educating believers on how to use a Bible concordance to study the Scriptures.
    b. Making sure the parking lot is properly striped and lit.
    c. Confronting ungodly spirits operating through people in the church.
    d. Teaching people how to deduct their tithe and offerings off their income tax.

9. When a fellow believer in your church family is *blatantly* and *deliberately* living in sin and has no intention of repenting and turning away from it, action must be taken. Read 1 Corinthians 5:1-11.

    a. What actions of *true love* should be taken by those in spiritual authority? What will happen if nothing is done?

    _____
    _____
    _____
    _____

b. What adjustments should *you* make in your relationship with this person?

c. Why should you treat unbelievers who are living in sin differently than a believer living in sin?

Encouragement from the COURAGEOUS

"The true man of God is heartsick, grieved at the *worldliness* of the church, grieved at the *blindness* of the church, grieved at the *corruption* in the church, grieved at the *toleration of sin* in the church, grieved at the *prayerlessness* in the church. He is disturbed that the corporate prayer of the church no longer pulls down the strongholds of the devil. He is embarrassed that the church folks no longer cry in their despair before a devil-ridden, sin-mad society. 'Why could we not cast him out?' God help us. (Matthew 17:19)."
—**Leonard Ravenhill**[7]

I [God] looked for someone who might rebuild the wall of righteousness that guards the land. I searched for someone to stand in the gap in the wall so I wouldn't have to destroy the land...
—**Ezekiel 22:30 NLT**
[Word in brackets added for clarity.]

10. As a parent, manager, teacher, church leader, government official or believer, you hold a position of authority. God is counting on *you* to help rebuild the wall of righteousness and stand in the gap in your sphere of influence. He wants you to *exercise* your authority—not *surrender* it to another.

    a. As a parent, what happens in your *home* when you abandon your place of authority?

b. What happens in a *church* when a pastor abandons his place of authority?

c. What happens in a *nation* when its leaders abandon their place of authority?

> **Fight** the good fight of faith, lay hold on eternal life, to which you were also called and have confessed the good confession in the presence of many witnesses.
> —**1 Timothy 6:12**
> [Boldness added for emphasis.]

11. John shared a story in chapter seven of his book about a woman at a church who got offended with his preaching and went home and "prayed against him." Knowingly or unknowingly, she became a vessel through which a spirit of intimidation was trying to *control* the pastor and the ministry of the church.

    a. Ask yourself: Do I regularly question or disagree with the decisions of my pastor, boss or spouse? Do I often seek to control the climate of my church, home or office? If so, why?

    b. In light of your previous answers, has a spirit of intimidation been operating through *you* and you have been unaware of it? What is the Lord showing you?

> "A person exercises **witchcraft** when he or she seeks to **control**. Yes, there is a form of witchcraft or control that conjures up demonic spirits. However, witchcraft is not limited to this."
> —**John Bevere** (page 71)

FAITH FACTOR
Intimidation is a spirit that seeks to control anyone and anything it can. As believers, we must *exercise* our God-given authority in our lives as well as our homes, churches and nation—confronting blatant, willful sin head on.

MAKE IT Real
RELATIONSHIP REVIEW

More than likely, you have experienced *being* intimidated, but have you ever been the one *doing* the intimidating? If you have been using intimidation to make others behave a certain way, you have *given place* to a spirit of intimidation. Knowingly or unknowingly, you have been in *partnership* with the enemy, and you cannot get delivered from something you are in agreement with—you cannot break free from someone with whom you are choosing to hold hands. This is what Paul meant when he said, "...I do not want you to *fellowship* and be *partners* with diabolical spirits..." (1 Corinthians 10:20 AMP). Once you sever the ungodly alliance with the adversary, you can experience true freedom.

> Take no part in and have no *fellowship* with the fruitless deeds and enterprises of darkness, but instead [let your lives be so in contrast as to] expose and reprove and convict them.
> —**Ephesians 5:11 AMP**
> [Italics added for emphasis.]

Take a few moments to review your relationships with your spouse, children, co-workers, church members, etc. Make a list of the people with whom you are in close relationship. Get gut-level honest with yourself and the Lord and ask yourself the following soul-searching questions.

WHICH RELATIONSHIPS DOES EACH QUESTION APPLY TO?
- Do any of these people seem to be afraid of me?
- Do *my* desires and decisions dominate my relationships?
- Do I tend to "steamroll" over others or use threats in order to get my way?
- When I interact with people, do I have a hidden agenda or an ulterior motive?
- Do I manipulate or control others by my emotional reactions or by withholding something?
- When I correct my children or others under my authority, do I use intimidation to get them to do something or change their behavior?
- Am I only concerned with seeing *my* plans fulfilled through my relationships, or am I equally concerned with seeing God's plans fulfilled in the lives of others too?

PERSON'S NAME   **WHAT GOD IS SHOWING ME ABOUT THIS RELATIONSHIP**

PRAYER OF REPENTANCE

Father, I repent for giving place to a spirit of intimidation. Please forgive me and wash me clean of the sin of using intimidation in my relationship with _____ (the person's name). I don't want to be in fellowship with the enemy—I choose to sever any partnership I have had with him. I don't want to be intimidated, and I don't want to intimidate others. Please give me the grace—the power of Your Holy Spirit—to recognize and resist any tendency to use intimidation to get my way or control situations and relationships. Thank You for showing me this powerful truth and setting me free. I ask You to bring healing to all of my relationships. Show me anyone You want me to apologize to, and give me the grace to do it. In Jesus' name, Amen.

THE CATASTROPHE OF COMPROMISE

> Like a muddied fountain and a polluted spring is a righteous man who yields, falls down, and **compromises** his integrity before the wicked.
> **—Proverbs 25:26 AMP**
> [Boldness added for emphasis.]

Have you ever asked questions like, "How far is *too* far? What can I watch and listen to and not sin? What places can I go and what things can I do and still be *OK* with God?" I think most of us have pondered questions like these at some point. Sadly, these are the symptoms of living life on the edge—*pushing the envelope* of pleasure to find out how far we can go and still be accepted by God.

Have you been there? Are you there right now? *Compromise*—it's one of the greatest temptations we face. It's the silent killer that slowly but surely sucks the life out of any believer who will give it the time of day. What is compromise? Basically, it is knowing in your heart what is right but choosing to go just below that standard. Every day people *rationalize* their actions in their mind and then compromise in their behavior. Consequently, it is destroying their lives and the lives of others.

RATIONALIZE

The word *rationalize* means "to make something that is irrational [illogical, foolish, crazy] appear rational or reasonable; to justify one's behavior or weaknesses, especially to oneself; to find plausible but untrue reasons for conduct."[8]

[Words in brackets added for clarity.]

Charles Swindoll is a seasoned pastor and best-selling author of many years. Carefully **read** this insightful excerpt from his book *Growing Strong in the Seasons of Life*, and ask the Holy Spirit to open your eyes to the grave danger of living life in the lethal lane of compromise:

"No family I know is interested in vacationing in a houseboat twenty feet above Niagara Falls. Or swimming in the Amazon near a school of piranhas. ...Or building a new home that straddles the San Andreas fault. ...I mean, some things make no sense at all. Like lighting a match to see if your gas tank is empty. Or stroking a rhino to see if he's tame. Man, that's lethal! They've got a name for nuts who try such stunts. Victims. Or (if they live to tell the story) just plain *stupid*.

And yet there's a strange species of Christian running loose today who flirts with risks far greater than any of the above. ...Who are they? They are the ones who rewrite the Bible to accommodate their lifestyle. We've all met them. From the skin out they have all the appearance of Your Basic Believer, but down inside, operation rationalization transpires daily. They are experts at rephrasing or explaining away the painful truth of the text. How do they think? Well, it's not very complicated. Whenever they run across Scripture verses or principles that attack their position, they alter them to accommodate their practice. That way, two things occur: (1) all desires (no matter how wrong) are fulfilled and (2) all guilt (no matter how justified) is erased.

...The simple fact is this: We reap *precisely* what we sow. If we sow a lifestyle that is more comfortable or easier or even happier—but is in direct disobedience to God's revealed Word—we ultimately reap *disaster*. It may not come soon...but it will come. And ...when the bills come due, the wages of willful sin are paid in full. God may seem slow. But He doesn't compromise with consequences."[9]

> Don't be misled; remember that you can't ignore God and get away with it: a man will always reap just the kind of crop he sows! If he sows to please his own wrong desires, he will be planting seeds of evil and he will surely reap a harvest of spiritual decay and death; but if he plants the good things of the Spirit, he will reap the everlasting life that the Holy Spirit gives him.
> **—Galatians 6:7-8 TLB**

Have you ever *purposely* compromised and went against what you knew in your heart was right? If yes, explain the situation and share what the Lord taught you through it.

_____
_____
_____
_____
_____
_____

Are you presently compromising in any area of your life? If so, where? What thoughts has the enemy fed your mind to get you to rationalize your actions?

_____
_____
_____
_____
_____
_____

Read Revelation 3:14-16. What word used in this passage describes a compromised life? How does God react to this condition? Are you in this condition?

_____
_____
_____
_____
_____

What's the Cure for Compromise? The strongest antidote against compromise is to be head over heels in love with the Lord. Nothing is greater. Having a fresh, personal awareness of God's passion for you and His deep desire to be your friend will move you away from the edge. Instead of wanting to see what you can get away with, you will want to get as far away from sin as possible. *Obedience* will become your heart's cry. Instead of feeling like you *have* to do what is right, you will *want* to do what is right. The question of *"How far is too far?"* will already be answered in your heart: Whatever you have *peace* about in your spirit, you can do. But anything you don't have peace about, you shouldn't do (see Colossians 3:15; Romans 14:23). And when in doubt, *don't!*

> "Intimidation paralyzes us in the realm of the spirit. It causes us to *compromise* what we know to be right. It causes us to allow or *tolerate* what we, under other circumstances, wouldn't stand for."
> **—John Bevere** (page 57)

Do you sense the conviction and correction of the Holy Spirit? If you do, don't take it as His disapproval—see it as a sign of His deep love. Scripture says, "…the Lord disciplines those He loves…God disciplines us for our good, that we may share in His holiness" (Hebrews 12:6,10 NIV). Take some time to sit quietly in the Lord's presence and repent of any compromise. Confront any area of sin in your life and ask God to forgive you and change you. Write out anything the Lord is specifically showing you or asking you to do.

_____
_____
_____
_____
_____
_____
_____
_____

1. *Standing Firm: 365 Devotionals to Strengthen Your Faith* (St. San Luis Obispo, CA: Parable) p. 226. 2. Adapted from two sources: *Thayer's Greek-English Lexicon of the New Testament*, Joseph H. Thayer (Grand Rapids, MI: Baker Book House Company, 1977) p. 523; *Vine's Complete Expository Dictionary of Old and New Testament Words*, W. E. Vine (Nashville, TN: Thomas Nelson, Inc. 1996) p. 593. 3. See note 1, p. 55. 4. Derek Prince, *Transformed for Life* (Grand Rapids, MI: Chosen Books, 2002) p. 86. 5. Adapted from *Merriam Webster's Desk Dictionary* (Springfield, MA: Merriam-Webster, Inc. 1995). 6. *Noah Webster's First Edition of an American Dictionary of the English Language* (1828), Republished in facsimile edition by Foundation for American Christian Education (San Francisco CA 1995). 7. See note 1, p. 283. 8. See note 5. 9. Charles R. Swindoll, *Growing Strong in the Seasons of Life* (Portland, OR: Multnomah Press, 1983) pp. 244-246.

Freedom Notes

"We need some Christians who will take up their cross daily, deny themselves and follow Christ. We don't need people making excuses for carnality—we need people who will say, 'I'm going to be **bold**, and I'm going to be **strong**.' Men and women, be strong *together*, in Jesus' name!"

—Lisa Bevere
(adapted from session 5)

Please refer to chapter 8 in the *Breaking Intimidation* book, along with session 5 of the teaching series.

Stir Up The Gift—*Power* 5

BOLDNESS

"Courage, bravery, fearlessness; freedom from timidity; liberty; confidence or confident trust." The general sense of the word *bold* is "open, forward, or rushing forward."[1]

"Boldness in itself is not a virtue, but *true boldness* is awakened in the life of a believer when he begins to realize that in him is a spirit of *power*, a spirit of *love* and a spirit of a *sound mind*. Those virtues will wake up the gift of God."
—**John Bevere** (adapted from session 5)

The wicked flee when no one pursues, but the righteous are *bold* as a lion.
—**Proverbs 28:1**
[Italics added for emphasis.]

1. While intimidation lulls the gift of God in us to sleep, *boldness* wakes it up. How can you obtain *true* boldness? It is birthed out of an ongoing, intimate relationship with the Lord. This includes having a rich understanding of His indestructible Word and being full of His all-powerful, life-giving Spirit. **Write out** and **hide in your heart** these core principles:

PSALM 27:4 — LET DAVID'S HEART CRY BE *YOUR* HEART CRY

_____

_____

_____

_____

JOSHUA 1:8 — LET JOSHUA'S KEY TO COURAGE BE *YOUR* KEY TO COURAGE

_____

_____

EPHESIANS 5:17-18 – LET PAUL'S DIRECTIVE TO THE EPHESIANS BE *YOUR* DIRECTIVE

2. Boldness in the life of a believer does amazing things. It provides the believer with a fearless motivation to move forward in the plan of God, and it sends a message to unbelievers as well.

   a. **Read** Joshua 2:8-11 and describe what boldness in the Israelites produced in the people of Jericho.

   b. **Read** Acts 4:1-13 and explain what the apostles' boldness enabled them to do *after* Jesus' resurrection that they were unable to do before it.

   c. What produced this boldness in them?

Check out
Acts 1:4-5, 8; 2:1-4; 4:29-31

> But if the Spirit of Him who raised Jesus from the dead dwells **in you**, He who raised Christ from the dead will also give life to your mortal bodies through His Spirit who dwells in you.
> —**Romans 8:11**
> [Boldness added for emphasis.]

Stir Up The Gift—*Power*

3. In Ephesians 1:17-20, 3:16-21 and Philippians 3:10, one of the things Paul repeatedly pursued and prayed for was that all believers would fully understand the invincible *power* of the Holy Spirit at work in us.

   a. What is your understanding of God's power in you, and why do you think it is important?

   _____
   _____
   _____
   _____
   _____
   _____
   _____

> ### *Encouragement* from the COURAGEOUS
>
> "Christ's indwelling in the human heart is the mystery of mysteries. ...When the Christian church realizes that they are the tangible, living, pulsating body—flesh and bones and blood and brain of Jesus Christ—and that God is manifesting through each one every minute and is endeavoring to accomplish His will for the world through them, not through some other body, then Christian service and responsibility will be understood."
>
> —John G. Lake[2]

   b. In what ways do you know *without a doubt* that God's power has changed your life?

   _____
   _____
   _____

   c. **Write out** and **hide in your heart** the word of the Lord to Zerubbabel and to *you*:

   ZECHARIAH 4:6

   _____
   _____
   _____
   _____

4. David was not a perfect man, but he was a man after God's heart. From his earliest years of tending his father's sheep, he also tended and enjoyed a close relationship with the Lord. The *boldness* he possessed was birthed out of intimately knowing God and His character.

Meditate on the message of these powerful passages from David:

The Lord is my **Shepherd** [to *feed, guide,* and *shield* me], I shall not lack.
—**Psalm 23:1 AMP**

The Lord is my **Light** and my **Salvation**—whom shall I fear or dread? The Lord is the **Refuge** and **Stronghold** of my life—of whom shall I be afraid?
—**Psalm 27:1 AMP**

The Lord is my **Strength** and my [impenetrable] **Shield**; my heart trusts in, relies on, and confidently leans on Him, and I am helped; therefore my heart greatly rejoices, and with my song will I praise Him.
—**Psalm 28:7 AMP**
[Italics and boldness added for emphasis.]

a. Based on your knowledge of Scripture and personal experience with the Lord, use your own words to complete this sentence: **The Lord is my** _____.

_____
_____
_____
_____

Write as many words that come to mind as you can.

b. These verses from the Psalms are not just for David—they are also for **you**. The Lord is *your* Shepherd, *your* Strength, *your* Refuge, *your* Stronghold, *your* Salvation and *your* impenetrable Shield. The question is: Do you believe it? If not, why?

_____
_____
_____
_____

For God shows no partiality [undue favor or unfairness; with Him one man is not different from another].
—**Romans 2:11 AMP**

"The devil knows who lives in you; he knows greater is He who is in you than he who is in the world (1 John 4:4), and I think his greatest fear is when a believer wakes up and realizes who they are in Christ Jesus."
—**John Bevere** (adapted from session 5)

5. One way Satan seeks to intimidate you is by constantly reminding you of past sins and present weaknesses. Through thoughts of *condemnation*, he attacks your mind by trying to make you feel so unworthy of the Lord's help that you give up praying altogether.

   a. As a believer, what does God say to you about condemnation?

   Check out Romans 8:1 and John 3:17-18

   b. Instead of being weighed down by guilt and condemnation and trying to be *good enough* to enter God's presence, what does He want you to do?

   Check out Hebrews 4:15-16 and Ephesians 3:12

Fascinating Fact
THE TRUE CHAMPION

The battle between David and Goliath in 1 Samuel 17 is an example of what was called "Battle of the Champions" in the ancient Near East. Instead of whole armies fighting, the strongest warrior of one nation would fight to the death the strongest warrior of the other. The victorious one would win victory for his entire army. Interestingly, this one-on-one combat was carried out based upon the belief that the gods of each army actually fought or decided the outcome of the battle. In David's battle against Goliath, both men called upon their god to empower them to defeat the other (see verses 43-47). David's victory over Goliath truly proved to all that the battle is the Lord's, and He is the true champion![3]

Encouragement from the COURAGEOUS

"*Goliath* isn't a Philistine word. It is actually a Hebrew word that means 'someone who wants to hold you down and strip you naked and enslave you.' In fact, the word *Philistine* is also a Hebrew word which means 'village dweller.' David knew that the real battle was with the *spirit of Goliath*—a spirit that wanted to *dwell in him*, to *enslave him*, and finally to *destroy him*."

—**Bob Katz**[4]

6. Before he physically fought the Philistine from Gath, David had to fight a spirit of intimidation on three different fronts—through Eliab, King Saul and Goliath himself. It's important to note that in each instance, David didn't just *think* about God's faithfulness—he opened his mouth and *spoke about it*.

   a. Instead of talking about what he saw in the natural—the size and experience of Goliath, the terror in his countrymen, etc.—on what did David focus his words?

   Check out 1 Samuel 17:45-47

   _____
   _____
   _____

   b. When *you* are faced with intimidating situations, what kind of words usually come out of your mouth? How does David's example challenge you to change?

   _____
   _____
   _____

   c. David *imitated* God by boldly declaring the end from the beginning—he called things that did not exist as though they already did (see Romans 4:17; Ephesians 5:1). Using familiar promises from God's Word and memories of His faithfulness to you, **write** a godly declaration to counteract the negative situation in which you find yourself right now.

   _____
   _____
   _____

> Death and life are in the power of (*your*) tongue, and they who indulge in it shall eat the fruit of it [for death or life].
> **—Proverbs 18:21 AMP**
> [Word in parentheses added for emphasis.]

WHAT'S IN A NAME?

A lot! And David was fully aware of the power and provision in the name of the Lord. "The name of the Lord is a *strong tower*; the righteous run to it and are safe" (Proverbs 18:10). Knowing God's name is knowing who He is and what is available to you through your covenant relationship in Christ. Every name given to God, as well as Jesus, is your place of safety, protection and provision.

Here are some of the names of the Lord, each describing a dimension of His awesome character. When doubt, anxiety, worry and fear come knocking at the door of your mind, run into the invincible, strong tower of His name—the name that is above every name! (See Philippians 2:9-10.) Open your mouth and *magnify the Lord*—declare who He is, and fear will be diminished.

Take time to meditate on the message of each name and personally proclaim who the Lord is to you.

NAME OF THE LORD	PERSONALIZED MEANING	SCRIPTURE REFERENCE
El Shaddai	The Almighty God is my all-sufficient supplier of needs.	Genesis 17:1-2
El Elyon	My God, the Creator of all things who is above all things.	Genesis 14:19
Jehovah-Jireh	The Lord is my provider.	Genesis 22:14
Jehovah-Rapha	The Lord is my healer.	Exodus 15:26
Jehovah-Nissi	The Lord is my banner of protection.	Exodus 17:15
Jehovah-Shalom	The Lord is my peace.	Judges 6:24
Jehovah-Rohi	The Lord is my Shepherd.	Psalm 23:1
Jehovah-Tsidkenu	The Lord is my righteousness.	Jeremiah 23:5-6

> O **magnify** the Lord with me, and let us exalt **His name** together. I sought (inquired of) the Lord and required Him [of necessity and on the authority of His Word], and He heard me, and delivered me from **all** my *fears*.
> **—Psalm 34:3-4 AMP**
> [Boldness and italics added for emphasis.]

7. Eliab and the army of Israel were under the power of a spirit of intimidation working through Goliath. When David *boldly* challenged the giant's taunts, he exposed the fear of Eliab and the Israelites. This made Eliab lash out at David in **anger**. His anger was the fruit of a root of fear.

   a. What was the real problem facing Eliab and Israel? Did Eliab's angry attack on David change the problem? What does this speak to you?

   b. Are you dealing with recurring bouts of explosive anger toward your spouse, children or someone else? If so, who are you really angry with, and what seems to *trigger* it?

   c. Chronic anger is often a sign of a spirit of fear at work. If you're dealing with anger, ask God to shine His searchlight of truth into your soul and reveal the real root. **Write** what He shows you.

> God's righteousness doesn't grow from human anger.
> —**James 1:20 The Message**

8. When an intimidated person is confronted, they look for a way of escape to release the pressure they're under. There is often something deep inside they would rather not face.

a. How does an intimidated person who is confronted usually react if they are *weak* in their soul? How about if they are *strong* in their soul?

b. What things do they often accuse the pure in heart of doing?

c. Why do people who are *impure*, negative and intimidated seek to intimidate people who are *pure*, positive and bold?

d. Do you find yourself doing any of these things? What is the Lord showing you?

9. The number one thing that will cause God to *resist* or *reject* a person is...

    a. Lack of love for others
    b. Being bound by a sinful habit
    c. Failure to pray and study the Word regularly
    d. An attitude of pride

Check out
Proverbs 3:34, James 4:6 and 1 Peter 5:5

> "It takes strong *women* to make strong *men*. When we talk about women being strong, we are not talking about women being strong at the *expense* of men. We don't need the men to be diminished by the women; we need the women to begin to build up the men—not dishonor, humiliate or demean them."
> **—Lisa Bevere** (adapted from session 5)

> And the Lord God said, "It is not good that man should be alone; I will make him a helper comparable to him."
> **—Genesis 2:18**

10. The greatest strength given to man apart from God Himself is woman. God divinely designed the two to be knitted together *heart to heart* and work together *hand in hand*.

    a. *Men*, how does your wife strengthen you and help bring out the boldness of the Lord?

    _____
    _____
    _____
    _____

    b. As a *husband*, have you recognized and received your wife's support and strength, or have you misread it as a threat and rejected it? Share your heart.

    _____
    _____
    _____
    _____

    c. *Women*, how have you offered strength and encouragement to your husband? If you have withheld it, why?

    _____
    _____
    _____
    _____

PONDER THESE PROMISES
GOD HAS GIVEN *YOU* POWER!

> But you shall receive *power* (ability, efficiency, and might) when the Holy Spirit has come upon you, and you shall be My witnesses in Jerusalem and all Judea and Samaria and to the ends (the very bounds) of the earth.
> **—Acts 1:8 AMP**

> Behold! I have given you *authority* and *power* to trample upon serpents and scorpions, and [physical and mental strength and ability] over all the power that the enemy [possesses]; and *nothing* shall in any way harm you.
> **—Luke 10:19 AMP**

> Have you not known? Have you not heard? The everlasting God, the Lord, the Creator of the ends of the earth, does not faint or grow weary; there is no searching of His understanding. He gives *power* to the faint and weary, and to him who has no might He increases *strength* [causing it to multiply and making it to abound].
> **—Isaiah 40:28-29 AMP**

> Blessed (happy, fortunate, to be envied) is the man whom You discipline and instruct, O Lord, and teach out of Your law, that You may give him *power* to keep himself calm in the days of adversity, until the [inevitable] pit of corruption is dug for the wicked.
> **—Psalm 94:12-13 AMP**

[Italics added for emphasis.]

11. God clearly communicates throughout His Word that He has given you authority and power over the enemy. How trustworthy is His Word? **Write out** and **hide in your heart** the answer to this question found in these related power passages:

    NUMBERS 23:19

Also
Check out
1 Kings 8:56

PSALM 12:6

Also **Check out** Psalm 18:30

PROVERBS 30:5

Also **Check out** Matthew 5:18

LUKE 21:33

"Intimidation is an enemy. It lies to you and says, 'I have more authority or power than you. You had better back off and do what I say! If you don't, you'll pay the consequences.' If we listen to these intimidating lies, the gift of God will go dormant, and we will live in an oppressed state. But when we *know* the One who has promised to be faithful, we can rest in the power that is above all other powers and, with David, face our giant of intimidation with great *boldness*."
—**John Bevere** (page 92)

Yet amid all these things we are *more than conquerors* and gain a surpassing victory through Him Who loved us.
—**Romans 8:37 AMP**
[Italics added for emphasis.]

FAITH FACTOR
While intimidation makes the gift and power of God in us become dormant, *boldness* stirs it up. True boldness is birthed out of an ongoing, intimate relationship with the Lord—a relationship in which you increasingly understand all that He is and all that you are in Him.

STIR UP THE GIFT—*POWER*

REMEMBER WHEN...

Next to the rich resource of God's Word and the unparalleled power of His Holy Spirit, nothing generates faith in you like *remembering when* God answered your prayers. Your personal experiences with the Lord are a very important part of your testimony—one of the weapons by which you overcome Satan (see Revelation 12:11).

Throughout the book of Psalms, a powerful picture is painted of the intimate relationship between God and David. Chapter after chapter, he voices his hopes and fears, joys and tears. Through it all—especially tough times—David recalls the track record of his faithful Father and Friend.

> I will remember the deeds of the Lord; yes, I will remember your miracles... ¹²Those wonderful deeds are constantly in my thoughts. I cannot stop thinking about them.
> **—Psalm 77:11-12**
> [Verse 11 taken from NIV; verse 12 from TLB.]

In a quiet place, away from the phone, email, television and other interruptions, pray and ask the Holy Spirit to bring to your remembrance some of the many mighty ways God has faithfully come through for you. Let Him take you on an eye-opening, faith-inspiring journey through the pages of your life, showing you the times He has answered your prayers. Here are some **points to ponder**...

REMEMBER WHEN GOD...
- Saved you and gave you eternal life
- Protected you from a serious accident
- Bailed you out of a major mess you made
- Healed you, your child, a close friend or family member
- Blessed you with a special friend when you really needed one
- Provided money to pay bills, buy food or erase an overwhelming debt
- Gave you wisdom and direction to make a very difficult and important decision
- Ministered through you to bring hope and healing to someone who desperately needed it

THE WORD OF **MY TESTIMONY**:

_____
_____
_____
_____
_____

PRAYER OF PRAISE AND THANKSGIVNG

O God! Your way is holy! No god is great like God! You're the God who makes things happen; You showed everyone what You can do—You pulled Your people out of the worst kind of trouble… (Psalm 77:13-14 The Message). *I bless the holy name of God with **all** my heart. Yes, I will bless the Lord and not forget the glorious things He does for me. He forgives **all** my sins. He heals me. He ransoms me from hell. He surrounds me with loving-kindness and tender mercies. He fills my life with good things! My youth is renewed like the eagle's!* (Psalm 103:1-5 TLB). *I will enter into His gates with thanksgiving and a thank offering and into His courts with praise! I will be thankful and say so to Him, I will bless and affectionately praise His name!* (Psalm 100:4 AMP). *Praise the Lord…Praise Him for His acts of power; praise Him for His surpassing greatness. Let everything that has breath praise the Lord. Praise the Lord!* (Psalm 150:1-2, 6 NIV).

EVERYBODY IS A BELIEVER?

> …"What are we to do, that we may [habitually] be working the works of God? [What are we to do to carry out what God requires?]" Jesus replied, "This is the work (service) that God asks of you: that you **believe** in the One Whom He has sent [that you cleave to, trust, rely on, and have faith in His Messenger]."
> **—John 6:28-29 AMP**
> [Boldness added for emphasis.]

Did you know that *everybody* is a believer? No kidding…it's true. Everybody is constantly putting their faith in something. Before you flip on a light switch, you *believe* the light is going to come on. Before you sit in a chair, you *believe* it is going to hold you and not fall apart. Before you pull out of your driveway and head for the supermarket, you *believe* the car is going to get you there. We are constantly believing in something, and what we believe in, we *act on*.

An atheist *believes* there is no God, and he lives his life accordingly. A Christian, on the other hand, believes there *is* a God, and Jesus is His Son; the only way to get right with Him and escape eternal punishment is to accept Jesus as Lord and Savior. So the question is not: *Are you a believer?* Rather, it's: *What are you believing in?*

BELIEVE

In most occurrences in the New Testament, the word *believe* is from the Greek word *pisteuo*, meaning "to be persuaded of, to place confidence in, to trust." In many cases, the word *believe* carries with it an active, ongoing quality of "believing or trusting."[5] This describes a person who is actively reaching forward *right now* to grab hold of what God has promised; his faith is in a state of consistently straining forward to take hold of a desired goal. When a person's faith is activated, it sets in motion supernatural *power* that enables him to do what would normally be impossible.[6]

Oswald Chambers was a Scottish Baptist minister who converted to Christ under the ministry of Charles Spurgeon. Carefully read this excerpt from his renowned book *My Utmost for His Highest*.

"Can you trust Jesus Christ where your common sense cannot trust Him? Can you venture heroically on Jesus Christ's statements when the facts of your common-sense life shout—'It's a lie'? On the mount it is easy to say—'Oh, yes, I believe God can do it'; but you have to come down into the demon-possessed valley and meet with facts that laugh ironically at the whole of your mount-of-transfiguration belief. Every time my programme of belief is clear to my own mind, I come across something that contradicts it. Let me say I believe God will supply all my need, and then let me run dry, with no outlook, and see whether I will go through the trial of faith, or whether I will sink back to something lower.

Faith must be tested because it can be turned into a personal possession only through conflict. What is your faith up against now? The test will either prove that your faith is right, or it will kill it. 'Blessed is he whosoever shall not be offended in Me.' The final thing is confidence in Jesus. **Believe** steadfastly *on Him* and all you come up against will develop your faith."[7]

The subject of faith and believing God is too vast to cover in a volume of books, much less a single devotional, but this should get you thinking and cause you to ask yourself: "What *am* I believing? Where am I placing my trust and confidence?" Clearly, what you are acting on is what you believe. You either believe and act on *God's Word*, or you believe and act on the *enemy's word* (which includes the voice of the world and the voice of your flesh through which Satan works). Indeed, as the Scripture says, "…man does not live on bread alone but on *every word* that comes from the mouth of the Lord" (Deuteronomy 8:3 NIV). Therefore, in every situation you face, make it a habit to get God's Word on it—find out what He's saying in the Scriptures and what He's confirming in your heart. Believe it. Act on it. Your faith will grow!

QUICK QUIZ

Check out
Romans 12:3

Where does faith—the ability to believe and trust—come from?

_____
_____

Check out
Romans 10:17,
Luke 8:15
and Jude 20

According to God's Word, how does your faith grow?

_____
_____
_____

How do life's experiences and God's Word work together to build your faith?

_____
_____
_____

What is the one thing upon which your faith should be built?

_____
_____
_____

Ask yourself, "Upon what am I basing my faith in God? Is my faith (confidence, trust) in God based on what I can see and hear? Is it based on my past experiences? Is it based on what has happened to others?" Get quiet and allow the Holy Spirit to show you your heart.

___

Now **faith** is the assurance (the confirmation, the title deed) of the things [we] hope for, being the proof of things [we] do not see and the conviction of their reality [faith perceiving as real fact what is not revealed to the senses]. ⁶It's impossible to please God apart from faith. And why? Because anyone who wants to approach God must believe both that he exists and that he cares enough to respond to those who seek him.
—**Hebrews 11:1,6**
[Boldness added for emphasis. Verse 1 taken from AMP; verse 6 is from The Message.]

Chew on These Mighty Morsels to Build Your Faith
Don't fear! God wants you to BELIEVE He is your...

PRESENT HELP	**PROVIDER**	**PROTECTOR**	**POWER SOURCE**
Joshua 1:5-9	Psalm 23:1;	Psalm 33:18-19;	2 Samuel 22:29-35
Isaiah 41:10,13;	34:10; 84:11	34:7	Psalm 28:7-8;
49:15-16	2 Corinthians	Psalm 91, 121	46:1-3
Jeremiah 1:7-8	9:8-11	Isaiah 54:17	Habakkuk 3:19
Acts 18:10	Philippians 4:19	Luke 12:7	2 Corinthians 12:9
	Hebrews 13:5-6		

God loves you with an intense, unconditional, everlasting love. Not only does He yearn to be welcome in your life, He also wants to em**power** you with the priceless gift of His Holy Spirit—the same gift He gave His disciples in the upper room on the day of Pentecost

Encouragement from the COURAGEOUS

"I think there can be no doubt that the need above all other needs in the church of God at this moment is the *power of the Holy Spirit*. More education, better organization, finer equipment, more advanced methods—all are unavailing. ...Good as these things are, they can never *give life*. 'It is the Spirit that quickeneth' [gives life – John 6:63]. Good as they are they can never bring power. 'Power belongeth unto God' [Psalm 62:11]. ...We may be sure of one thing, that for our deep trouble there is no cure apart from a visitation, yes, an *invasion of power* from above."

—**A.W. Tozer**[8]

[Words in brackets added for clarity; italics for emphasis.]

(see Acts 2:1-4). If you're a believer and have never asked the Father to give you the baptism of His Spirit, I encourage you to do so. Jesus said in Luke 11:13 that if we, being as imperfect as we are, know how to give good gifts to our children, how much more will our heavenly Father give the Holy Spirit to those who ask Him? If you *have* received the gift of God's Spirit, but the surge of His power in your life has been diminished, ask the Father to unlock the fountain of living water within you and restore a fresh flow!

Take time to write what the Lord is showing you, as well as what you are experiencing in His presence.

_____
_____
_____
_____
_____
_____
_____
_____
_____
_____
_____

---

1. *Noah Webster's First Edition of an American Dictionary of the English Language* (1828), Republished in facsimile edition by Foundation for American Christian Education (San Francisco, CA 1995). 2. John G. Lake, *Spiritual Hunger, The God-Men and Other Sermons* (Dallas, TX: Christ for the Nations, Inc. 1979) pp. 29, 30. 3. Adapted from "Battle by Champions," *NIV Archeological Study Bible* (Grand Rapids, MI: The Zondervan Corporation, 2005) p. 422. 4. Bob Katz, "David Knew What Goliath Meant," *Enjoying Everyday Life* Magazine (Fenton, MO: Joyce Meyer Ministries, September 2006) p. 16. 5. Adapted from *Vine's Complete Expository Dictionary of Old and New Testament Words*, W. E. Vine (Nashville, TN: Thomas Nelson, Inc. 1996) p. 61, New Testament Words. 6. Adapted from Rick Renner's book, *Sparkling Gems from the Greek* (Tulsa, OK: Teach All Nations, 2003) p. 781. 7. Oswald Chambers, *My Utmost for His Highest* (Uhrichville, OH: Barbour Publishing, Inc. 1997) p. 242. 8. A.W. Tozer, *A Treasury of A.W. Tozer* (Harrisburg, PA: Christian Publications, Inc. 1980) pp. 61, 62.

Freedom Notes

"What you need to do is put your will completely into the hands of your Lord, surrendering to Him the entire control of it. Say, 'Yes, Lord, YES!' to everything, and trust Him to work in you to will, as to bring your whole wishes and affections into conformity with His own sweet and lovable, and most lovely will. It is wonderful what miracles God works in wills that are utterly surrendered to Him. He turns hard things into easy, and bitter things into sweet. It is not that He puts easy things in the place of the hard, but He actually changes the hard thing into an easy one."

—**Hannah Whitall Smith**[1]

Please refer to chapters 9 and 10 in the *Breaking Intimidation* book, along with session 6 of the teaching series.

STIR UP THE GIFT—*LOVE* | 6

> "You can be outgoing, strong, bold—even anointed—and still fight intimidation. When the pressure becomes strong enough, what you're made of is exposed. Possessing a spirit of timidity has nothing to do with a deficiency in personality, physical strength or anointing."
>
> —**John Bevere** (page 98)

1. Without question, Peter was strong and seemingly fearless. His life gives us a powerful example of the *two* types of boldness a person can have: He displayed a *false* boldness before the crucifixion and a *true* boldness after the day of Pentecost. Explain the difference between the two, showing what each is built on.

   _____
   _____
   _____
   _____

2. Peter's boldness to strike out against the Roman soldiers and Jewish leaders in the Garden of Gethsemane was drawn partially from pride, as well as a desire to win the approval and admiration of the other disciples.

   a. Whose approval and admiration mean the most to you? How often do you seek it?

   _____
   _____
   _____
   _____

b. Get quiet before the Lord: Read each person's name from your previous answer and ask the Lord to show you *why* you desire and seek their approval.

_____
_____
_____
_____

Encouragement from the COURAGEOUS

"Human compliments are like perfume. Smell them, enjoy them while they last. Please don't drink them; they will poison you."

—**Anonymous**[2]

There's trouble ahead when you live only for the *approval of others*, saying what flatters them, doing what indulges them. Popularity contests are not truth contests—look how many scoundrel preachers were approved by your ancestors! Your task is to be *true*, not popular.

—**Luke 6:26 The Message**
[Italics added for emphasis.]

3. Identifying your true *motives* is very important. They are the "why" behind the "what"—they are the reasons that motivate you to do everything you do. On the surface, Peter and the other disciples seemed bold and motivated by love for Jesus. But when the heat was on, their true colors were revealed.

Check out
Luke 22:24

a. At the Last Supper, what were the disciples' true motives for trying to determine who would betray Jesus?

_____
_____
_____
_____

b. According to Philippians 2:3-4, what types of things should *never* motivate you? How will these same things affect your prayers? (See James 4:1-3.)

_____
_____
_____
_____

c. **Write out** and **hide in your heart** Hebrews 4:12, revealing the number one weapon for exposing the hidden motives, attitudes and intents of your heart.

If possible, use an Amplified Bible for writing out this verse.

> We justify our actions by appearances; God examines our *motives*. Clean living before God and justice with our neighbors mean far more to God than religious performance. *Mixed motives* twist life into tangles; *pure motives* take you straight down the road.
> —**Proverbs 21:2-3, 8 The Message**
> [Italics added for emphasis.]

4. Gethsemane, a name meaning "oil press," was a place of intense pressure for Jesus and the disciples. Under intense pressure, what is inside your soul—what you really *want*, *think* and *feel*—is forced out into the open.

    a. Describe the difference between the way Jesus responded to the pressure of Gethsemane and the way His disciples responded. What did the pressure reveal in each of them?

    b. As a believer, you probably know that God uses trials and troubles to mold us into His image. Describe an intense trial you have gone through or are currently going through.

    c. What attitudes, emotions or motives you didn't know existed have been brought to the surface of your life by the pressure of the situation?

> ### FASCINATING FACT
> **SWEATING BLOOD: A PHYSIOLOGICAL PHENOMENON**
>
> Sweating drops of blood—is it possible? According to medical science, it is. The clinical term for the condition is called *hematohidrosis*. Around the sweat glands, there are numerous blood vessels that form a net-like structure. When a person is under an enormous amount of stress, pressure is placed on these vessels causing them to constrict. Then as the anxiety passes, the blood vessels dilate to such a degree that they actually burst, releasing blood into the sweat glands. As the glands produce a lot of sweat, they push the blood to the surface of the skin—forming droplets of blood mixed with sweat. Interestingly, the physician Gospel writer, Luke, was the only one to mention this physiological phenomenon. Indeed, Jesus experienced tremendous agony in His soul while praying in Gethsemane—not just because of the physical torture He would soon endure, but also because He was about to take the full weight of all mankind's sin and sickness upon Himself. This would result in a temporary separation from the Father, a form of hell itself that He had never experienced. But he did it out of His immeasurable love for you and me.[3]

5. The greatest eye-opening revelation you can receive while in the "oil press" of testing is to discover which person you love more: *yourself* or *God*.

   a. What did Jesus' deep love for the Father help Him conquer that no man had conquered before?

   b. If you are filled with *fear* or are under a spirit of intimidation, who or what are you focusing on? If you are filled with God's *love*, who or what are you focusing on?

c. Describe a situation in which you struggled greatly between doing *your* will and God's will, but in the end chose to do what God asked. How did things turn out?

___

___

___

___

> I am able to do nothing from Myself [independently, of My own accord—but only as I am taught by God and as I get His orders]. Even as I hear, I judge [I decide as I am bidden to decide. As the voice comes to Me, so I give a decision], and My judgment is right (just, righteous), because *I do not seek or consult My own will* [I have no desire to do what is pleasing to Myself, My own aim, My own purpose] but only the will and pleasure of the Father Who sent Me.
>
> **—John 5:30 AMP**
> [Italics added for emphasis.]

6. Jesus told His disciples repeatedly that He was going to die at the hands of the Pharisees. Yet, for some reason they were unable to hear Him. Their hearts were so sold on the idea of Jesus establishing a *physical* kingdom on the earth at that time that when He was arrested and crucified, they were devastated.

   a. Have you ever strongly believed or expected that God was going to do something and then it never happened or something drastically different took place? What was it?

   ___

   ___

   ___

> **Encouragement from the COURAGEOUS**
>
> "The Bible is the story of two gardens. Eden and Gethsemane. In the first, Adam took a fall. In the second, Jesus took a stand. In the first, God sought Adam. In the second, Jesus sought God. In Eden, Satan led Adam to a tree that led to his death. From Gethsemane, Jesus went to a tree that led to our life."
>
> **—Max Lucado**[4]

b. How has the unexpected chain of events affected your walk with the Lord?

> "You can be really bold when you know God is doing exactly what you think He's going to be doing, but when the tables are turned and things start happening differently than what you expected, what you are made of really comes out."
> —**John Bevere** (adapted from session 6)

7. When Jesus went to the Cross, He won *your* battle; when He was in the Garden, He won *His* battle. In the midst of tremendous pressure and sorrow, He fought fiercely for three hours to *lose His life* to the will of the Father. He gave us an example of what we must do daily—die to our will.

   READ LUKE 9:23-26 AND LUKE 14:26-27.

   a. In what ways have you *lost your life* for the sake of Jesus? How have you *denied* yourself and *taken up your cross* to follow Him?

   b. In what areas has it been hard to lose your life and deny yourself? Write them out and surrender them to the Lord in prayer.

   c. When Jesus says you must *hate* your father, mother, brothers, wife and children in order to be His disciple, what does this mean to you personally?

> I have been crucified with Christ: and I myself no
> longer live, but *Christ lives in me*. And the real life
> I now have within this body is a result of my *trusting in
> the Son of God*, who loved me and gave himself for me.
> —**Galatians 2:20 TLB**
> [Italics added for emphasis.]

8. Dying daily to *our* will includes dying to sin—especially those sins that we so easily give in to and are entangled by.

    a. **Write out** and **hide in your heart** these challenging truths:

    ROMANS 6:11-13

    _____
    _____
    _____
    _____

    HEBREWS 12:1

    _____
    _____
    _____
    _____

    b. Name some of the sins that *used to* easily entangle you but don't anymore.

    _____
    _____
    _____
    _____

    c. List some of the sins (ungodly tendencies) you are currently working to break free from.

    _____
    _____
    _____
    _____

> "When we truly lay down our lives out of love for Jesus, we will no longer care what happens to us because we know we are committed into His care. Then we are dead and hidden in Him (Colossians 3:3). We do not need to worry because our lives are no longer our own, but His. He purchased us; therefore, whatever happens to us is His concern only. We just love and obey."
> **—John Bevere** (page 105)
> [Scripture reference added.]

> Casting the whole of your care [all your *anxieties*, all your *worries*, all your *concerns*, once and for all] on Him, for He cares for you affectionately and cares about you watchfully.
> **—1 Peter 5:7 AMP**
> [Italics added for emphasis.]

9. As much as we would like to avoid temptation altogether, we can't. It's a part of life that all of us must face. The Bible says in Hebrews 4:15 that Jesus was tempted in *every* way as we are and yet was without sin.

   Check out Matthew 6:13 and Luke 22:40,46

   a. Instead of praying that you are never tempted, how does Jesus instruct you to pray?

   _____
   _____
   _____
   _____

   b. Learning from Jesus' example in Luke 4:1-13, how are you to respond to temptation?

   _____
   _____
   _____
   _____
   _____
   _____
   _____
   _____
   _____

Encouragement from the COURAGEOUS

"The reason why many fail in battle is because they wait until the hour of battle. The reason why others succeed is because they have gained their victory on their knees long before the battle came...Anticipate your battles; *fight them on your knees before temptation comes*, and you will always have victory."

—R. A. Torrey[5]
[Italics added for emphasis.]

10. There is subtle but deadly danger in depending on your *own* strength to serve and obey the Lord and escape the enemy of fear.

   a. What does Paul say in Philippians 3:3 about putting confidence in your own abilities?

   b. Read Jeremiah 17:5-8. Describe what will happen if you trust in man (including yourself) and what will happen if you trust in the Lord.

   c. **Write out** and **hide in your heart** these related power principles:

   ROMANS 7:18

   JOHN 6:63

> ### Encouragement from the COURAGEOUS
>
> "Trust in yourself and you are doomed to disappointment...but trust in God, and you are never to be confounded in time or eternity."
> —**Dwight L. Moody**[6]

> He who trusts in himself is a fool, but he
> who walks in wisdom is kept safe.
> **—Proverbs 28:26 NIV**

11. When we are faced with fear, temptation or a test of any kind, our number one response should always be to *run to the Lord for His grace*. Yes, grace is the undeserved favor of God, but it is also the divine **power of the Holy Spirit** readily available to any believer who will humbly ask for it (see James 4:6 below).

    Check out 2 Corinthians 12:7-10

    a. When Paul was in the midst of a severe trial, he sought God to take away the demonic attack. What did God tell him? What does this example speak to you personally?

    _____
    _____
    _____
    _____

    b. When you are in a severe spiritual attack, what is normally your first response? What adjustments is the Holy Spirit asking you to make?

    _____
    _____
    _____
    _____

    c. **Write out** 1 Corinthians 15:10 and **make it your own**:

    1 CORINTHIANS 15:10

    _____
    _____
    _____
    _____

> But He gives us more and more grace (**power of the Holy Spirit**,
> to meet this evil tendency and all others fully). That is why He says,
> God sets Himself against the proud and haughty, but gives grace
> [continually] to the lowly (those who are humble enough to receive it).
> **—James 4:6 AMP**
> [Boldness added for emphasis.]

Prayer of Surrender

"Lord, I am no longer my own, but Yours. Put me to what You will, rank me with whom You will. Let me be employed by You or laid aside for You, exalted for You or brought low by You. Let me have all things, let me have nothing, I freely and heartily yield all things to Your pleasure and disposal. And now, O glorious and blessed God, Father, Son, and Holy Spirit, You are mine and I am Yours. So be it. Amen."

—John Wesley[7]

FAITH FACTOR

The *love of self* is the root of intimidation and fear. The only way to truly conquer intimidation is to lose your life—surrender yourself and all your hopes, plans and dreams to the hands of the Lord and allow His everlasting, all-powerful love to be *perfected* in you.

THAT'S ENTERTAINMENT?

Probably the greatest fear man has to deal with is the fear of death, especially a violent death at the hands of a killer. The irony of this fact, however, is that many of the same people who battle with the fear of being killed will often sit and watch a movie filled with violent killings—all in the name of "entertainment." Hollywood has made multiple millions off of many "thriller-killer" films, featuring the butchering of the human body. Without question, Satan himself is behind the production of this mode of media. Why does the devil delight in depicting the destruction of the human body? Because our body is the very temple of the living God.

> …For we are the *temple of the living God*. As God said: "I will live in them and walk among them. I will be their God, and they will be my people. Therefore, come out from among unbelievers and separate yourselves from them, says the Lord. **Don't touch their filthy things**, and I will welcome you. And I will be your Father, and you will be my sons and daughters, says the Lord Almighty."
> —2 Corinthians 6:16-18 NLT vs.2
> [Italics and boldness added for emphasis.]

In the *Make It Real* activity of chapter 4, we examined the vital importance of not being in *partnership* or agreement with the enemy. When you make the choice to watch a *movie*, listen to *music*, play a *video game*, or read a *book* that features the violent destruction of the human body, you are welcoming the fear of death into your life. *Buying* these forms of entertainment gives fear an even more permanent place in your home. Like the landing lights on an airport runway, having these types of "entertainment" sends a signal to the spirit of fear to *come in for a landing* in your life.

Pray and ask the Holy Spirit to show you any questionable movies, music, video games, books, etc. that are in your possession feeding the spirit of fear in you; ask Him for the grace to get rid of them and the wisdom to find something better for you and your family.

I believe the Holy Spirit is showing me I need to **Clean Out My Closet** and get rid of…

MOVIES

_____
_____
_____
_____
_____
_____
_____

MUSIC

_____
_____
_____
_____
_____
_____
_____

VIDEO GAMES

_____
_____
_____
_____
_____
_____
_____

BOOKS/OTHER

_____
_____
_____
_____
_____
_____
_____

Note: Don't give any of these things away to be a stumbling block for someone else; trash them or burn them.

PERFECT, BOUNDLESS LOVE

> See what [an incredible] quality of **love** the Father has given (shown, bestowed on) us, that we should [be permitted to] be named and called and counted the children of God! And so we are!
> —1 John 3:1 AMP

Love—it's not a feeling. It's an *action*! In John 3:16, one of the classic quotes of the Christian faith, Jesus declares that "God so *loved* the world that He **gave** His only begotten Son, that whoever believes in Him should not perish but have everlasting life." His love is displayed in His giving. Romans 5:8 goes on to say that "…God demonstrates His own love toward us, in that while we were still sinners, Christ died for us." Again, God's boundless love is made visible and tangible through His giving.

Not only does God *show* us His love through giving us Jesus, but He also *gives* us love itself. Romans 5:5 proclaims that "…God's *love* has been poured out in our hearts through the Holy Spirit Who has been given to us" (AMP). The love that God gives is unequivocally special. It is *agapao* love—love that is *all-powerful*, *unconditional*, *indestructible*, *selfless* and *everlasting* (just to name a few). In fact, the love that God has poured out into our hearts is *everything* God is. Why? Because **God is love** (see 1 John 4:16). Love is not just something He does—it's who He *is*.

> …**God is love**, and he who dwells and continues in love dwells and continues in God, and God dwells and continues in him. In this [union and communion with Him] love is brought to *completion* and attains *perfection* with us, that we may have confidence for the day of judgment [with assurance and boldness to face Him], because as He is, so are we in this world. *There is no fear in love* [dread does not exist], but full-grown (*complete, perfect*) love turns fear out of doors and expels every trace of terror! For fear brings with it the thought of punishment, and [so] he who is afraid has not reached the full maturity of love [is not yet grown into love's complete perfection].
> —1 John 4:16-18 AMP
> [Boldness and italics added for emphasis.]

PERFECT

"To finish or complete so as to leave nothing wanting; to give to any thing all that is necessary to its nature and kind; to instruct fully and make fully skillful."[8]

Read 2 Corinthians 3:18 and Romans 1:17 and give the two phrases Paul uses to describe your spiritual growth. How do you think this relates to the fruit of God's love poured out in your heart?

According to 1 John 4:17-18, how is God's love *made perfect* in you?

In your own words, describe God's love that is at work *in* you and *through* you.

How do you *know that you know* that God loves you?

Complete the thought: "It is hard for me to believe God loves me when…"

Surrender these doubts and fears to the Father in prayer. Ask Him for a deeper revelation of His love in these areas.

According to Romans 8:35-39, what things cannot separate you from the love of God?

_____
_____
_____
_____
_____

PRAYER FOR A REVELATION OF GOD'S LOVE

Dear Heavenly Father,

*Give me a deeper revelation of Your unconditional, everlasting love for me, and may I be rooted deeply and securely in it. May I have the power and be strong to understand with all believers the breadth and length and height and depth of Your love for me. Lord, let it not just be a head knowledge, but a heart revelation that I really come to know, practically and through experience with You. May Your love be **perfected** in me more and more with each passing day, and may Your perfect love push out of my life every trace of fear. In Jesus' name, Amen!*

[Prayer based on Ephesians 3:17-19 AMP.]

"My friends, we have not even begun to fathom the breadth and the length and the height and the depth of the love and majesty of God. He is the Alpha and Omega, the beginning and the end. Circumstances will not dictate the days of your life, God will. God, in His *boundless love*, will carry you safely Home into eternity in His glorious presence."

—**Sheila Walsh**[9]
[Italics added for emphasis.]

"Men and women of God, now you know the truth: The only way to conquer intimidation is to *lose your life*. Cry out to God as you read. Don't draw back but dare to believe. Ask Him to fill your heart with this love—His love, the kind that never withdraws. Ask Him for His grace to overcome the obstacles you face. Ask Him to grant you the privilege of going into the hard places. Pray to be on the cutting edge of what He is doing in the earth. Don't ask for a life of ease. Instead ask for one that glorifies Him."

—**John Bevere** (pages 118, 119)

After completing this week's lesson, what is the Holy Spirit showing you about your level of love for *God* and for *yourself?* Ask yourself some soul-searching questions: *Who am I more loyal to and in love with? Why am I serving Jesus? Is it because of what I can get from Him and what He can do for me? Or, do I love and serve Him out of a grateful heart for who He is and all He's done for me?* Get quiet before the Lord and allow His Spirit to show you your heart; write what He reveals. Remember, there is no condemnation for you in Christ Jesus. Understanding His love for you is a *progressive* revelation. You won't "arrive" until you arrive in heaven.

---

1. Quotes on *Submission and Surrender to Christ* (www.dailychristianquote.com, retrieved 9/2/08). 2. Quotes on *Pride and Humility*, see note 1. 3. Adapted from "Did Jesus Really Sweat Drops of Blood?" Paul S. Taylor of Eden Communications (http://christiananswers.net/q-eden/edn-t018.html, retrieved 9-2-08). 4. Max Lucado, *The Greatest Moments in the Life of Christ* (Nashville, TN: J. Countryman, 1998) p. 95. 5. Quotes on *Spiritual Warfare* (www.dailychristianquote.com, retrieved 8/8/08). 6. Quotes on *Trusting God in Times of Trial*, see note 1. 7. See note 1. 8. *Noah Webster's First Edition of an American Dictionary of the English Language* (1828), Republished in facsimile edition by Foundation for American Christian Education (San Francisco, CA 1995). 9. Patsy Clairmont, Barbara Johnson, Marilyn Meberg, Luci Swindoll, Sheila Walsh, and Thelma Wells, *Boundless Love* (Grand Rapids, MI: Zondervan, 2001) p. 250.

Freedom Notes

"I believe God has to accomplish a certain work in us before we can lay claim to any covenant promise. What is this precedent work, upon which all others depend? The prophet Jeremiah tells us: '...I will put my fear in their hearts, that they shall not depart from me' (Jeremiah 32:40). God's precedent work of the covenant is to put *His fear* in our hearts, by the work of the *Holy Spirit*. ...We can't work up a holy fear by ourselves. We can't obtain it by the laying on of hands or the strivings of our flesh. No—the only way this holy work can be accomplished in us is if *God's Spirit* performs it."

—**David Wilkerson**[1]

Please refer to chapters 11, 12 and 13 in the *Breaking Intimidation* book, along with session 7 of the teaching series.

Stir Up The Gift—*Sound Mind* | 7

> "You will serve and obey whom you fear! If you fear man, you will serve him. If you fear God, you will serve Him. You cannot fear God if you fear man because you cannot serve two masters (Matthew 6:24)! On the other hand, you will not be afraid of man if you fear God!"
> —**John Bevere** (page 129)

> All has been heard; the end of the matter is: **Fear God** [revere and worship Him, knowing that He is] and keep His commandments, for *this is the whole of man* [the full, original purpose of his creation, the object of God's providence, the root of character, the foundation of all happiness, the adjustment to all inharmonious circumstances and conditions under the sun] and the whole [duty] for every man.
> —**Ecclesiastes 12:13 AMP**
> [Boldness and italics added for emphasis.]

1. It is very important for you to understand the differences between the *fear of man* and the *fear of God*. Carefully read the detailed descriptions of each found on page 128. Then, in your own words, write out their meanings, along with what results from doing each one.

   FEAR OF MAN

   _____
   _____
   _____
   _____
   _____

FEAR OF GOD

Which one do you tend to do more? What evidence in your life supports this?

> ### Encouragement from the COURAGEOUS
>
> "...The fear of the Lord isn't an outdated concept belonging in the dusty archives of hellfire and brimstone preachers: 'The fear of the Lord is clean, enduring forever' (Psalm 19:9). This important theme occurs consistently throughout Scripture, from Genesis 20:11 to Revelation 19:5. Fearing God is not a law-based principle, but rather it is an eternally enduring aspect of our relationship to God."
> —Neil T. Anderson & Rich Miller[2]

2. To better determine how much you fear the Lord, take some time to evaluate your relationship with Him. Ask yourself...

   a. "What's my attitude toward God—honor and reverence or dishonor and familiarity?"

   b. "What kind of *thoughts* and *words* about God fill my mind and mouth—especially in the midst of trials?"

STIR UP THE GIFT—*SOUND MIND*

c. The fear of God draws you *toward* Him; the fear of man causes you to *withdraw* from Him. Where do you feel more comfortable—in God's presence or the presence of men? Why?

_____
_____
_____
_____

d. "How do I act in church during the message, at offering time and during the altar call? Do I show up late and miss worship? Do I leave early to avoid the crowded parking lot and get to lunch?"

_____
_____
_____
_____

> "The only way to walk totally free from intimidation is to walk in the *fear of the Lord*. The Bible says, 'In the fear of the Lord there is *strong confidence*' (Proverbs 14:26). Strong confidence produces the *boldness* we need to go God's way rather than man's way. …If we do not grow in the fear of the Lord, we risk the danger of becoming *familiar* with God and treating as common the things He considers holy."
> —**John Bevere** (pages 128, 134)

3. Isaiah 11:3 says that Jesus Himself *delighted* in the fear of the Lord. As we seek to understand and grow in the fear of the Lord, our lives will be bountifully blessed. Look up the Scriptures below and write the blessings that the fear of the Lord will bring you:

SCRIPTURE REFERENCE	FEARING THE LORD WILL BLESS MY LIFE BY…
Proverbs 1:7; 9:10	Bringing me knowledge and wisdom.
Proverbs 8:13	Enabling me to hate evil.
Proverbs 14:26	Providing me a refuge or fortress of protection.
Proverbs 14:27	Becoming a fountain of life for me.
Proverbs 15:33	Teaching me wisdom.
Proverbs 16:6	Helping me avoid evil.
Proverbs 19:23	Adding life to me.
Proverbs 22:4	Bringing me wealth, honor and long life.

> My child, listen to me and treasure my instructions. Tune your
> ears to wisdom, and concentrate on understanding. Cry out
> for insight and understanding. Search for them as you would
> for lost money or hidden treasure. Then you will understand what
> it means to fear the Lord, and you will gain knowledge of God.
> **—Proverbs 2:1-5 NLT**

4. "Fearing people is a dangerous trap, but to trust the Lord means safety" (Proverbs 29:25 NLT). If you are ensnared by the fear of man, you will seek to be accepted and seen as "normal" by others—even at the expense of offending God. **Write out** these words of warning from Scripture, declaring the danger of trying to *fit in* with the world.

JOHN 15:19

_____
_____
_____

JAMES 4:4

_____
_____
_____

1 JOHN 2:15

_____
_____

> Friends, this world is not your home, so don't make yourselves
> cozy in it. Don't indulge your ego at the expense of your soul.
> **—1 Peter 2:11 The Message**

> "We can easily fear God while He is doing miracles and demonstrating
> of His power. But God is looking for those who will also reverence
> and fear Him when they do not perceive His presence or power,
> like children who obey even when their father is not watching. The
> truly obedient are so when no one is around to monitor them."
> **—John Bevere** (page 138)

5. It's easy to get excited and give God praise when He is *visibly active* in your life. However, when hardships hit and He seems to be silent, praising and trusting Him becomes a sacrifice and requires steadfast faith.

   a. If you are living an *obedient* life before God and He seems to be silent, what is He actually saying to you?

   _____
   _____
   _____
   _____

   b. Intimidating circumstances and people often pressure us and make us feel like we have to "do something" when life seems to be coming apart at the seams. Describe a situation like this in your life and the outcome of your efforts. What did you learn as a result?

   _____
   _____
   _____
   _____

   > …Blessed (happy, fortunate, to be envied) are all those who [earnestly] wait for Him, who expect and look and long for Him [for His victory, His favor, His love, His peace, His joy, and His matchless, unbroken companionship]!
   > **—Isaiah 30:18 AMP**

6. One thing you definitely don't want to do when God's presence and power aren't apparent is *complain*. Israel murmured and complained, and it cost them greatly. Complaining communicates a lack of fear of the Lord and also a love of self.

   a. How do you feel when your children or grandchildren whine and complain about being "bored" or "never getting to do anything" after you've just done a lot for them?

   _____
   _____
   _____
   _____

b. How do you think our heavenly Father feels when we complain to Him after all He's done for us?

c. **Write out** and **hide in your heart** these power principles to help you live a healthy life:

1 THESSALONIANS 5:16-18

PHILIPPIANS 2:14

Also **Check out** 1 Corinthians 10:9-11; 1 Timothy 6:6-8

Encouragement from the COURAGEOUS

"Until the will and the affections are brought under the authority of Christ, we have not begun to understand, let alone to accept, His lordship."

—**Elisabeth Elliot**[3]

> A simple life in the Fear-of-God is better than a rich life with a ton of headaches.
> —**Proverbs 15:16 The Message**

7. Having a healthy fear of the Lord includes not only understanding that He is merciful and loving, but also that He is holy and just. To focus *only* on His goodness and omit His righteous judgment is to have an unhealthy, unbalanced image of who God is.

a. What will understanding God's *goodness* produce in your life? What will happen if you *only* consider His goodness?

b. What will understanding God's *righteous judgment* produce in your life? What will happen if you *only* consider His righteous judgment?

c. As a believer, Jesus Christ is your *Savior*, but He also wants to be your *Lord*. The question is: What evidence proves that Jesus is *Lord* of your life?

> Therefore I remind you to stir up the gift of God which is in you through the laying on of my hands. For God has not given us a spirit of fear, but of *power* and of *love* and of a **sound mind**.
> —**2 Timothy 1:6-7**
> [Italics and boldness added for emphasis.]

A Lesson in Greek

"This phrase [sound mind] is taken from the Greek word *sophroneo*, which is a compound word combining *sodzo* and *phroneo*. The Greek word *sodzo* means to be *saved* or *delivered*. It suggests something that is *delivered, rescued, revived, salvaged*, and *protected* and is now *safe and secure*.

...The second part of the phrase 'sound mind' comes from the Greek word *phroneo*, which carries the idea of a person's *intelligence* or *total frame of thinking*—including his *rationale, logic* and *emotions*. The word *phroneo* refers to *every part of the human mind, including all the processes that are engaged in making the mind function and come to conclusions*.

When the words *sodzo* and *phroneo* are compounded into one word, they form the word *sophroneo*, which pictures *a mind that has been delivered, rescued, revived, salvaged and protected and is now safe and secure*. Thus, even if your mind is tempted to

> succumb to fear, as was the case with Timothy, you can allow God's Word and the Holy Spirit to work in you to deliver, rescue, revive and salvage your mind.[4]
>
> ...As we obey the Word of God and listen to the Holy Spirit's leading, we will have wisdom to know every step we need to take in the days ahead. ...There is no doubt that we are living in some of the most challenging days the world has ever seen. But you can face these times victoriously because God has given you a *sound mind*; He has given you the promises of His Word; and He has given you the leadership of His Spirit."[5]
>
> **—Rick Renner**

8. A *sound mind* is the third key ingredient needed in overcoming a spirit of intimidation. Soundness of mind is not just an in-depth knowledge of the Scriptures. A sound mind comes from knowing the mind of Christ—knowing what His Spirit is saying *right now*.

   a. The Pharisees had great knowledge of the Scriptures but didn't know the *spirit* or *heart* behind them. This became deadly for them and those they led. What do you think having only head knowledge of God's Word will produce in you?

   _____
   _____
   _____
   _____
   _____

   Check out
   2 Timothy
   2:15;
   3:16-17

   b. If only having knowledge of the Scriptures can lead to problems, why is it still valuable and vital for you to study God's Word?

   _____
   _____
   _____
   _____
   _____

c. How will you know *the mind of Christ* in a situation—how does the Holy Spirit work with the Word?

Check out
John 16:13-14

_____
_____
_____
_____

"Jesus declared, 'Man shall not live by bread alone, but by every word that proceeds from the mouth of God' (Matthew 4:4). Notice He did not say 'proceeded.' That would be past tense. The Scriptures alone are what *proceeded* out of the mouth of God. He said 'proceeds,' which is present tense. We must know the Lord of the Scriptures to know what is *proceeding* out of His mouth today."
—**John Bevere** (pages 158, 159)

> *Encouragement from the* **COURAGEOUS**
>
> "I seek the will of the Spirit of God through, or in connection with, the Word of God. *The Spirit and the Word must be combined.* If I look to the Spirit alone without the Word, I lay myself open to great delusions. If the Holy Spirit guides us, He will do it *according to the Scriptures* and never contrary to them."
>
> —**George Muller**[6]
> [Italics added for emphasis.]

9. Having a sound mind is one of the wonderful blessings that comes with fearing the Lord. Like David, the fear of the Lord will enable you to *act* and not *react* in high-pressure situations.

   a. **Read** 1 Samuel 13:5-14; 15:18-24. What did King Saul do under pressure that you should *never* do? What motivated him to do what he did?

   _____
   _____
   _____
   _____

   b. From David's example in 1 Samuel 23:1-4; 30:6-8, what is the *first* thing you should always do when you need direction and help?

   _____
   _____
   _____

c. **Write out** and **hide in your heart** this divine invitation for revelation on what to do.

JAMES 1:5

_____
_____
_____
_____

10. God doesn't want you to be anxious or worried about how you will respond to others or be intimidated by them—regardless of who they are. He has given you a sound mind, the mind of Christ, to effectively handle any situation you face.

    a. According to Luke 12:11-12 and Matthew 10:19, what are you promised when you find yourself in confrontation with others?

    _____
    _____
    _____
    _____

    b. Carefully read and meditate on 1 Corinthians 2:11-16 and explain what having the *mind of Christ* enables you to do.

    _____
    _____
    _____
    _____

> "A *sound mind* knows what God is saying and doing *right now*. Only the Spirit of God can reveal this. He may communicate by Scripture; He may speak the word to my heart by an inward knowing or in His still, small voice. When we know what God is saying, we are founded on an unshakable rock."
> **—John Bevere** (page 162)

11. Many of the Pharisees genuinely believed they were right—that Jesus was not the Messiah. Why? Because He didn't fit into their mental "box" of what they understood the Messiah to be in Scripture. Their confidence was in their *own understanding* of the Scriptures—not the Lord.

a. In whom are you placing your confidence—yourself and your knowledge of the Word, or in Christ? How often do you seek God's direction when making decisions?

b. **Read** Simeon's story in Luke 2:25-32. Explain what repeatedly dominated and motivated his life—even in going to the temple the day Jesus was dedicated.

c. **Write out** and **hide in your heart** these powerful promises from God to direct your life:

PROVERBS 3:5-8

JOHN 16:13-14

> **FAITH FACTOR**
> Through our faith in Jesus Christ, we are given the gift of a *sound mind*, or the *mind of Christ*. As we grow in the fear of the Lord, our fear of man will diminish and our spirit will become more and more in tune with the voice of God's Spirit. We will seek and find the word of the Lord and know what to say and do in any situation in which we find ourselves.

THINK *FAST!*

Have you ever gotten a stubborn stain on your clothes that just wouldn't come out? More than likely, you put a special stain remover on it, gave it some time to soak and then washed it again. In a similar way, you may be dealing with a stubborn sin that has stained your soul and you just can't seem to break free from it. In this situation, declaring a *fast* may be just what you need.

In Matthew 17, there is a story of a father who brought his demon-possessed son to the disciples to be delivered. When they were unable to deliver him, the father cried out to Jesus for help. After Jesus set the man's son free, the disciples asked Jesus why they were unable to do it. Jesus said, "...this kind does not go out except by prayer and *fasting*" (Matthew 17:21 AMP).

Although you may not hear much about fasting these days, it is still a *very important* part of a believer's life. In essence, a fast is an intentional decision to abstain from eating food in order to gain spiritual benefits. You can fast all food or certain types of food, as well as activities you really enjoy. Basically, your fast says to God (and to yourself), "Lord, I want Your help in this area of my life more than I want the pleasure of eating food or doing this activity."

If you are struggling with certain fears, a negative attitude or some other type of ungodly thinking or behavior you want to see change, ask the Lord if He is calling you to a fast at this time. (see Joel 1:14; 2:12).

What Will Fasting Produce in You?
- An increased hunger for intimacy with the Father.
- An increased sensitivity and ability to hear God speaking to you.
- An increased fullness of God's manifest power working in and through your life.
- Ultimately, fasting increases your spiritual capacity, giving your spirit the upper hand over your flesh. Very often you will also experience a breakthrough in difficult circumstances and deliverance from wrong mindsets and habits that have held you hostage.

Consider Fasting from...
- One or more of your favorite foods (coffee, candy, bread, etc.) for a set period of time.
- All foods except fruits and vegetables.
- Entertainment (television, movies, music, talk radio, Internet, etc.).

Pray and ask the Lord to show you if and what you should fast. Write below what He reveals to you. Ask the Lord for His *grace* to stay committed to the fast and dedicate the time you would be eating to praying and studying the Word.

DATE STARTED _____   DATE COMPLETED _____

My Plan to Fast:

_____
_____
_____
_____
_____

Remember to Pen Your Progress at the end of the chapter. Write out what the Lord does in your life as a result.

A Breath of Fresh *Prayer*

> …The earnest (heartfelt, continued) prayer of a righteous man makes tremendous power available [dynamic in its working].
> —**James 5:16 AMP**

PRAYER—a topic that you have probably heard multiple messages on or even read about in books. To some, prayer seems to be a deep, mystical practice performed in a certain posture or place. But the truth is, prayer is simply *talking to God* and *listening as He talks to you*. That's it. There are a number of types of prayer, but in its purest form, prayer is ongoing, *unbroken* communion and fellowship with your heavenly Father.

Indeed, prayer is not a once a month, once a week or once a day *event*. Prayer is meant to be a *lifestyle*. Smith Wigglesworth said, "I don't often spend more than half an hour in prayer at one time, but I never go more than half an hour without praying."[7] You can, and should, pray anywhere, anytime, about anything. This is what Paul means when he says to *pray without ceasing* (1 Thessalonians 5:17). God, the Almighty Creator of heaven and earth, wants you to experience prayer like *breathing*—as a seemingly effortless, instinctive part of your everyday life that you can't live without.

Encouragement from the COURAGEOUS

"The soul which has come into intimate contact with God in the silence of the prayer chamber is never out of conscious touch with the Father; the heart is always going out to Him in loving communion, and the moment the mind is released from the task upon which it is engaged, it returns as naturally to God as the bird does to its nest. What a beautiful conception of prayer we get if we regard it in this light."

—E.M. Bounds[8]

Get quiet before the Lord and answer these questions honestly:

What is prayer to you? How would you describe your prayer life?

___

Is something blocking the flow of fellowship with your heavenly Father? Is there anything keeping you from praying anytime, anywhere, about anything? If so, what is it?

___

In regard to prayer, how would you like to see your communion with the Father grow in the next year?

___

My friend, God—your heavenly Father—loves you *passionately*. He robbed heaven of the richest resource in the universe—Jesus—to ransom your life from the enemy and restore you to unbroken, ongoing fellowship with Himself. Scripture says, "...The Spirit Whom He has caused to dwell in us yearns over us and He yearns for the Spirit [to be welcome] with a *jealous love*" (James 4:5 AMP). Indeed, the Holy Spirit is God's gift to you—to guide you into *all* truth and teach you *all* things (see John 16:13; 14:26). He is speaking, and you can hear Him!

> "The Holy Spirit has been sent to speak to us. What does He speak? Whatever He hears He speaks. That's why we've got to have a vibrant relationship with the Holy Spirit because we can never know the mind of Christ unless we know how to hear the voice of the Spirit."
> —**John Bevere** (adapted from session 7)

Meditate on the Message

…[Jesus'] sheep hear his voice and come to him; and he calls his own sheep by name and leads them out. He walks ahead of them; and they follow him, for they recognize his voice. They won't follow a stranger but will run from him, for they don't recognize his voice. My sheep recognize my voice, and I know them, and they follow me.

—**John 10:3-5, 27 TLB**
[Word in brackets added for clarity.]

…You have given me the capacity to hear and obey [Your law, a more valuable service than] burnt offerings and sin offerings [which] You do not require.

—**Psalm 40:6 AMP**

And your ears will hear a word behind you, saying, This is the way; walk in it, when you turn to the right hand and when you turn to the left.

—**Isaiah 30:21 AMP**

As a believer, you are one of Jesus' sheep and can hear His voice. Take a moment to reflect on your walk with God. What are some of the ways the Holy Spirit has spoken to you?

_____
_____
_____
_____
_____
_____
_____

Not only can you hear God's voice, *He also hears your voice*. Carefully read the verses below and write what the Holy Spirit reveals to you about God's ability and desire to hear you:

Psalm 4:3; 18:6; 34:15-18; 91:14-16 • Proverbs 15:29 • Isaiah 65:24 • 1 Peter 3:12

_____
_____
_____
_____
_____
_____

One of the most common prayers we pray is for *God's direction* in the decisions we make. This divine wisdom is the *mind of Christ*, or *word of the Lord*, we desperately need to live our lives. **Write out** and **hide in your heart** these powerful promises from your heavenly Father to you:

PSALM 25:9,12

_____
_____
_____
_____
_____
_____
_____

PSALM 32:8

_____
_____
_____
_____
_____
_____

Just like He did with Adam and Eve before the fall, God wants to walk with you and talk with you—He wants to hear what's on your heart and share with you what's on His heart. Our privilege to pray—to stay connected in unbroken fellowship with the Father—is not based on what we do; it's based on what Jesus *did*. The closer your relationship is with the Father, the freer you will feel to share *everything* with Him—your fears and tears, your hopes and dreams, as well as your sins that need to be washed away. Go ahead—take a *deep breath of fresh prayer*!

> The secret [of the sweet, satisfying companionship] of the Lord have they who fear (revere and worship) Him, and He will show them His covenant and reveal to them its [deep, inner] meaning.
> **—Psalm 25:14 AMP**

PRAYER OF DEDICATION

Father, thank You for this session on the power of a sound mind. I humbly ask You to develop a sound mind in me—that I might have the mind of Christ *and know what to do in any situation I face. Forgive me for leaning on my own understanding and for falling into the trap of the fear of man. The only one I want to reverentially fear is You. You know what is best for my life—not me or anyone else. Give me a renewed hunger for You and Your Word. Holy Spirit, when I sit down to read and study the Scriptures, please let it come alive; reveal the Word of the Lord to me that I might have the sound mind of Jesus Christ in me. I totally submit myself to you. Lead me and direct me into all truth. In Jesus' name, Amen.*

Pen Your PROGRESS

> "When our spirits are filled with *power, love* and *the word of the Lord* [having a sound mind], we will not fall prey to intimidation. It is not just one of these virtues but the combination of all three that undergirds us. Paul would have listed only one if that was all it took. To walk in godly boldness, it takes all three."
> **—John Bevere** (page 154)
> [Words in brackets added for clarity.]

What is the Holy Spirit speaking to your heart through this week's challenging study? *Get quiet* before the Lord and ask Him to show you any area where you have "boxed Him in." Ask Him to *break the box* and invite Him to do exceedingly, abundantly above and beyond all that you dare to ask or think! Write down the thoughts and feelings of your soul and spirit and anything the Holy Spirit is showing you or asking you to do.

---

1. David Wilkerson, *The New Covenant Unveiled* (Lindale, TX: Wilkerson Trust Publications, 2000) p. 69. 2. Neil T. Anderson & Rich Miller, *Freedom from Fear* (Eugene, OR: Harvest House Publishers, 1999) p. 236. 3. Quotes on *Submission and Surrender to Christ* (www.dailychristianquote.com, retrieved 9/2/08). 4. Rick Renner, *Sparkling Gems from the Greek* (Tulsa, OK: Teach All Nations, 2003) p. 73. 5. See note 3, p. 997. 6. Quotes on *Guidance and Direction* (www.dailychrisitianquote.com, retrieved 9/11/08). 7. Quotes by Smith Wigglesworth, see note 6. 8. Quotes by E.M. Bounds, see note 6.

Freedom Notes

"...I will not in any way fail you nor give you up nor leave you without support. [I will] not, [I will] not, [I will] not in any degree leave you helpless nor forsake nor let [you] down (relax My hold on you)! [Assuredly not!]"

—**God, *Your Heavenly Father***
Hebrews 13:5 AMP

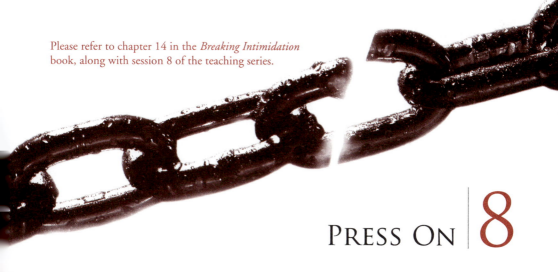

Please refer to chapter 14 in the *Breaking Intimidation* book, along with session 8 of the teaching series.

Press On | 8

What then shall we say to [all] this? If God is for us, who [can be] against us? [Who can be our foe, if God is on our side?]
—**Romans 8:31 AMP**

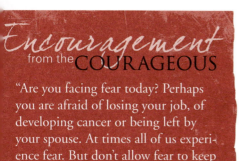

"Are you facing fear today? Perhaps you are afraid of losing your job, of developing cancer or being left by your spouse. At times all of us experience fear. But don't allow fear to keep you from being used by God. He has kept you thus far; trust Him for the rest of the way."

—**Woodrow Kroll**[1]

1. Moses was *called by God* to deliver the children of Israel. Nehemiah was *called by God* to rebuild the walls of Jerusalem. And Jesus was *called by God* to preach the good news of the kingdom of God. Yet, all these men, and many others, faced tremendous *opposition* while accomplishing their task.

   a. According to James 1:2-4 and 2 Corinthians 4:17, how should you view opposition?

   b. If you run from intimidating people or situations, what will eventually happen? Have you ever experienced this? If so, share what happened.

c. Look up these powerful promises in a few different versions of the Bible. **Write out** each in the version that touches your heart most deeply.

Check out www.biblegateway.com for multiple versions of God's Word

GALATIANS 6:9

_____
_____
_____

HEBREWS 10:36

_____
_____
_____

JAMES 1:12

_____
_____
_____

> "...the purpose of intimidation: to weaken us so we cannot accomplish the will of God and will no longer resist the intimidator. If we do not *stand against this steadfastly*, we will succumb. Our enemy, the devil, attempts many different avenues of intimidation when we invade his territory. He doesn't try once and then give up. If he can stop, postpone or weaken us, then he keeps the kingdom of God from advancing."
> —**John Bevere** (page 180)

2. Nehemiah was given authority by King Artaxerxes to return to Judah and rebuild the walls of Jerusalem. As he and the Israelites were exercising their authority, their enemies repeatedly attempted to intimidate them and stop them from completing what they were called to do.

   a. What task(s) has the Lord called you to and given you authority to carry out, yet the enemy has persistently tried to stop you from doing?

   _____
   _____
   _____

b. Name three tactics of intimidation the enemy has often used against you.

c. How is this lesson helping you see and recognize the *enemy's attacks* of intimidation, as well as the *purposes of God*, in a whole new light?

DISCOURAGE

The opposite of *courage* is *discourage*, which means "to extinguish the courage of; to dishearten; to depress the spirits; to deprive of confidence." When someone is discouraged they are deterred, prevented or frightened from taking on a task or responsibility.[2]

Check out the definitions of *courage* and *encourage* in chapter 3.

> "We need to treat *discouragement* as an enemy. We underestimate its power to prevent us from obtaining the high calling of God. If God tells Joshua seven times to be strong and courageous, then we must take heed also. Discouragement is a killer! If not confronted, it will cause us to draw back and keep us from fulfilling God's will."
> —**John Bevere** (adapted from page 184)

3. Discouragement, threats and distractions—all strategically used by Satan to terrify you with intimidation and sidetrack you from carrying out what the Lord has called you to do.

    a. What things do you frequently face that *discourage* you and drain you of strength to fulfill your calling?

b. Name a few of the most deadly *distractions* Satan has repeatedly placed in your path.

_____
_____
_____
_____

c. What angry *threats* has he often whispered in your ear that cause you to freeze in fear?

_____
_____
_____
_____

Do as Nehemiah did! Every time opposition raises its ugly head, earnestly seek the Lord in prayer—for grace to overcome intimidation and the mind of Christ to know what to do (see James 1:5; 4:6). As you pray, surrender to Him each distraction and discouragement, each angry threat of wrath and harm, and each slanderous accusation and lie as they come. God will ignite His fire of courage and boldness in you to overcome!

Encouragement from the COURAGEOUS

"Courage is contagious. When a brave man takes a stand, the spines of others are often stiffened."
—Billy Graham[3]

4. To counter and combat the damaging schemes and attacks of the enemy, you must identify and incorporate into your life the relationships and things that inspire courage, faith and boldness and help you stay focused on the Lord and the task He has called you to.

   a. List some of the things that ignite a fire of *boldness*, *bravery* and *courage* in you.

_____
_____
_____
_____
_____

b. Who do you hang around with who encourages you to *grow in your faith* and *not give up* when times are tough?

OPPRESSION

The word *oppress* literally means "to press." *Oppression* is "the infliction of unreasonable burdens; a sense of heaviness or weight in the breast; overburdened, misery, hardship, calamity, depression, dullness of spirit."[5]

5. Satan would love nothing more than to see us separated from God forever. But if he can't take us to hell with him, he certainly doesn't want us taking anyone to heaven with us. Through *oppression*, a spirit closely related to intimidation, he seeks to make our lives miserable.

> ### Encouragement from the COURAGEOUS
>
> "I had *feelings of fear* about the future...The devil kept on whispering, 'It's all right now, but what about afterward? You are going to be very lonely'....And *I turned to my God* in a kind of desperation and said, 'Lord, what can I do? How can I go on to the end?' And He said, 'None of them that trust in Me shall be desolate.' That word has been with me ever since."
>
> —**Amy Carmichael**[4]
> [Italics added for emphasis.]

a. Carefully read the definition of *oppression* and ask yourself: *In what ways have I tolerated and become comfortable with feelings of oppression?*

b. You have been given a powerful weapon against oppression —the garment of praise! **Write out** and **hide in your heart** these proclamations to praise the Lord:

PSALM 100:4

_____
_____
_____
_____

PSALM 149:1

_____
_____
_____
_____

HEBREWS 13:15

_____
_____
_____
_____

> "God is not pleased when you tolerate what He has paid a high price to deliver you from. What you don't confront will not change. As believers we sometimes think, 'Well, if I just ignore it, it'll go away.' No. No confrontation, no change. What you confront with *godly confrontation* will change."
> **—John Bevere** (adapted from session 8)

Not that I have already obtained all this, or have already been made perfect, but I **press on** to take hold of that for which Christ Jesus took hold of me. Brothers, I do not consider myself yet to have taken hold of it. But one thing I do: Forgetting what is behind and straining toward what is ahead, I *press on* toward the goal to win the prize [of the high calling] for which God has called me heavenward in Christ Jesus.
—Philippians 3:12-14 NIV
[Words in brackets from KJV; italics and boldness added for emphasis.]

6. In Philippians 3, Paul talks about pressing toward the high calling in Jesus Christ. Indeed, there is both a high calling and a low calling in Him.

   a. Describe what it means to live in the *high calling* of Christ and what comes with the territory.

   b. Explain the reasons why many Christians settle for living in the *low calling*.

   c. Revisit John's vision and analogy comparing the opposition we face in the high calling with rowing a boat against the current of a fast-flowing river. What does this speak to you personally?

   d. Which of the two callings do you generally live in? What things in your life confirm this?

> "The enemy wants to sidetrack us to make us ineffective in our labor. Satan will not try this only once. He is persistent. We must be stronger in our resolve than he is in his. That is why the Bible says we are to 'resist him, steadfast in the faith' (1 Peter 5:9). The word *steadfast* means 'strong, firm and immovable.' Too many people give up after a few hits from the enemy rather than remaining immovable until the victory is complete."
> —**John Bevere** (page 178)

7. If you are *stronger in God* than an unbeliever is in sin, what will happen? Give a few examples of people in your life—past or present.

8. Sometimes we need wisdom to deal with situations that do not have a clear-cut answer in Scripture. In cases like these, we need to follow the godly instructions given in Colossians 3:15 and Romans 14:23. **Meditate on the message** of these verses, and then, in your own words, write the general rule of thumb given in each for making decisions.

> And let the *peace* (soul harmony which comes) from Christ rule (*act as umpire* continually) in your hearts [deciding and settling with finality all questions that arise in your minds, in that peaceful state] to which as [members of Christ's] one body you were also called [to live]. And be thankful (appreciative), [giving praise to God always].
> —**Colossians 3:15 AMP**

> But anyone who believes that something he wants to do is wrong shouldn't do it. He sins if he does, for he thinks it is wrong, and so for him it is wrong. Anything that is done apart from what he feels is right [faith] is sin.
> —**Romans 14:23 TLB**
> [Word in brackets added for clarity.]

DISCERNMENT

To *discern* means "to separate or distinguish; to see and understand the difference between two or more things; to make a distinction, as to *discern* between good and evil, truth and falsehood."[6] *Discernment* uses the eyes and mind; and in the case of *spiritual discernment*, the power of the Holy Spirit dwelling within man's spirit enables him to discern whether a spirit operating through another is of God or Satan.[7]

9. When the disciples asked Jesus about the sign of His return and the end of the age, the *first* thing Jesus said was "…Take heed that no one *deceives* you" (Matthew 24:4). In these last days, we desperately need spiritual discernment—it's the only thing that will empower us to discover and defeat the intimidating deception the enemy brings.

   a. Nehemiah had discernment—even in recognizing the sly scam of a fake friend's prophecy. Has the enemy ever used someone you knew to give you "a word" to try and take you away from your task? Explain the situation and how you handled it.

   b. According to Isaiah 11:2-3, Jesus operated in the gift of discernment. **Write out** verse 3 and **claim it as your own**.

   ISAIAH 11:3

c. First Corinthians 12:10 identifies *discernment* as a gift of the Spirit. Carefully read 1 Corinthians 2:10-16 and write what the Lord reveals to you about this powerful gift.

___

> Is the gift of discernment operating in your life? If it isn't or you desire to walk in a deeper dimension of discernment, pray and ask the Lord to awaken a new level of His Spirit within you.

> Dear friends, do not believe everyone who claims to speak by the Spirit. You must test them to see if the spirit they have comes from God. For there are many false prophets in the world. ²Here's how you test for the *genuine Spirit of God*. Everyone who confesses openly his faith in Jesus Christ—the Son of God, who came as an actual flesh-and-blood person—comes from God and belongs to God. ³And everyone who refuses to confess faith in Jesus has nothing in common with God. This is the spirit of antichrist that you heard was coming. Well, here it is, sooner than we thought!
> **—1 John 4:1-3**
> [Verse 1 taken from NLT vs.2; verses 2 and 3 taken from The Message.]

10. Just as God works through people to do good, the enemy works through people to plot and plan evil. Sanballat, Tobiah and Geshem are perfect examples. **Read** Psalm 2:1-6; 37:9-13 and Micah 2:1-3 to answer these questions.

    a. Describe how God responds to the evil plots of man.

    ___

    b. How does the Lord want you to respond when the wicked seem to flourish?

    ___

c. What will happen to the wicked and those who plot evil against His righteous people?

> ### Encouragement from the COURAGEOUS
>
> "Christianity never was designed by God to make a lot of weaklings. It was designed to bring forth a race of men who were *bold*, *strong*, *pure* and *good*. The greatest and strongest and noblest is always the humblest. …God is endeavoring by His Spirit in these days to exalt the souls of men into that *high place*, that holy life, that heavenly state whereby men walk day by day, hour by hour in the heavenly consciousness of the *presence of Christ*."
>
> —**John G. Lake**[8]

11. Ultimately, gaining and maintaining a *strong spirit* is the weapon that will keep you free from the paralyzing clutches of fear. How do you gain and maintain a strong spirit? By staying intimately connected to Christ. Through an ongoing relationship with Him, you'll grow in the fear of the Lord, as well as His love, grace, wisdom and all that He is.

a. What was the reason God repeatedly told Joshua to be *strong* and *courageous*?

Check out Joshua 1:7

b. As a strong *soldier of the Cross*, you must be prepared for battle. Carefully read 1 Peter 4:1-2, and ask the Holy Spirit to reveal to you what it means to *arm yourself* to suffer in the flesh.

c. **Write out** and **hide in your heart** these powerful promises encouraging you to be strong in spirit:

2 TIMOTHY 2:1

_____

_____

_____

1 CORINTHIANS 16:13

_____

_____

_____

PHILIPPIANS 1:27-28

_____

_____

_____

_____

> The Lord God is my *Strength*, my *personal bravery*, and my *invincible army*; He makes my feet like hinds' feet and will make me to walk [not to stand still in terror, but to walk] and make [spiritual] progress upon my high places [of trouble, suffering, or responsibility]!
> —**Habakkuk 3:19 AMP**
> [Italics added for emphasis.]

FAITH FACTOR

God is always *for you* and *with you*. He has called you to do certain things and given you the authority and power to carry them out. Stay focused. Stay strong. Press past the tactics of intimidation and opposition Satan puts in your path. Your life will be rewarded if you don't give up!

WHERE YOUR ATTENTION GOES, THE **POWER** FLOWS!

For as [a man] thinks in his heart, so is he.... [Therefore] keep and guard your heart with all vigilance and above all that you guard, for out of it flow the springs of life.
—**Proverbs 23:7; 4:23 AMP**
[Words in brackets added for clarity and flow.]

As a believer, God Himself desires to direct your daily decisions by the power and wisdom of His Holy Spirit. Unfortunately, there are a number of other voices competing for your attention—especially the media. Just as our bodies are built by the physical food we eat, our souls and spirits are built by the things we allow to enter our eyes, ears and mind. The question is: What are you "chewing" on in your mind and spirit? What you are full of is going to dominate and dictate the thoughts you think, the words you speak, and the actions you take.

Take a few moments to reflect upon an average week in your life and estimate how much time you invest in these activities.

NON SPIRIT-BUILDING ACTIVITIES	
Watching television	
Listening to talk radio/secular music	
Surfing the Internet	
Watching movies (rented or in the theater)	
Reading (books, magazines, newspapers, etc.)	
Total Time Invested (approximate) =	

SPIRIT-BUILDING ACTIVITIES	
Reading, studying, meditating on God's Word	
Praying—including praising, worshipping and sitting quietly in God's presence	
Fellowshipping with believers (at church, in small groups, etc.)	
Watching/Listening to teaching (CDs, DVDs, TV, radio, Internet, etc.)	
Reaching out to others (witnessing in deed and in word)	
Total Time Invested (approximate) =	

Which area gets more of your time and attention—*non spirit-building* activities or *spirit-building* activities? Consequently, which holds a stronger influence in your life?

Finish the statement: "The three *most important* activities in my life that I can't live without are…"

1.
2.
3.

What do these answers say to you about the condition of your heart and loyalty to the Lord?

Take a few minutes to pray and ask the Holy Spirit to show you what adjustments He wants you to make in your life. Cry out for His grace (strength) to make them. **Write** what He reveals.

EXERCISE!

> ...Exercise daily in God—no spiritual flabbiness, please! Workouts in the gymnasium are useful, but a disciplined life in God is far more so, making you fit both today and forever. You can count on this. Take it to heart.
> **—1 Timothy 4:7-9 The Message**

When does an athlete need to be in his best physical shape? Just before his toughest competition. In the same way an athlete exercises his body to get in shape physically, the Lord desires His body to exercise and get in shape spiritually. The truth is, the body of Christ is spiritually out of shape, and our toughest competition is just ahead.

In essence, *exercise* means to **train**, **discipline** and **practice habitually**.[9] That is what an athlete does—he *trains* in his sport, he *disciplines* his body, and he *practices habitually* so when he faces his competition, he is ready. When we exercise physically, we get physically fit; when we exercise spiritually, we get spiritually fit. The question is: Are you exercising your faith?

> ...employ every effort in exercising your faith to develop virtue (excellence, resolution, Christian energy), and in [*exercising*] virtue [develop] knowledge (intelligence), and in [*exercising*] knowledge [develop] self-control, and in [*exercising*] self-control [develop] steadfastness (patience, endurance), and in [*exercising*] steadfastness [develop] godliness (piety), and in [*exercising*] godliness [develop] brotherly affection, and in [*exercising*] brotherly affection [develop] Christian love.
> **—2 Peter 1:5-7 AMP**

EXERCISING SPIRITUALLY = LIVING LIKE CHRIST

For Further Study
What are some of the specific ways the LORD **requires you to exercise your faith?**

Colossians 3:12-14	1 Peter 3:11	1 Thessalonians 5:16
Acts 24:16	Proverbs 4:23	John 13:34
Romans 12:18	Ephesians 4:32	Ephesians 4:26-27
2 Timothy 1:6		

Check out
Philippians
1:6; 2:13; 1
Thessalonians
5:23-24;
Hebrews
13:20-21

Philippians 2:12 says to "…**work out** your own salvation with fear and trembling." Where do you get the strength to *work out* spiritually?

What are the benefits of exercise? **Write out** Hebrews 12:11 for the answer.

If you're like most people, you probably don't like to exercise. **Think**: What is it about exercising physically that people dislike so much? How does this compare with exercising your faith?

Exercise *strengthens* weak areas and helps maintain and make stronger areas that are already in shape. What weaknesses has the Lord revealed to you in your thinking, speaking, emotional responses and decision making?

Weight training offers a powerful parallel between the benefits of physical exercise and spiritual exercise. From the bench *press* to the leg *press* to the military *press*, each workout embodies Paul's challenge of *pressing* toward the mark of the high calling. Check out the chart below; carefully read each element of exercise and its physical purpose, then answer how you think it applies to exercising your faith.

ELEMENT OF EXERCISE	ITS PHYSICAL PURPOSE	HOW DO YOU THINK THIS APPLIES TO *SPIRITUAL EXERCISE*?
CONCENTRATION	Focused effort to develop certain muscles.	
SETS or CYCLES	A series of repetitious movements designed to build specific muscles; sets allow a period of rest between exercises.	
REPETITION	A movement performed over and over designed to strengthen the muscles, bones and body.	
RESISTANCE	To withstand the force of; to fight against. Resistance begins light and is gradually increased over time. The heavier the resistance, the greater the strength that is developed.	
PAIN	Exercise produces muscle fatigue and soreness. But once rested, muscles heal and are strengthened. No pain, no gain.	

> …God is strong, and he wants **you** strong. So take everything the Master has set out for you, well-made weapons of the best materials. And put them to use so you will be able to stand up to everything the Devil throws your way. This is no afternoon athletic contest that we'll walk away from and forget about in a couple of hours. This is for keeps, a life-or-death fight to the finish against the Devil and all his angels.
> —**Ephesians 6:10-12 The Message**
> [Boldness added for emphasis.]

RECOMMENDED READING
Dressed to Kill—a Biblical Approach to Spiritual Warfare and Armor by Rick Renner, published by Teach All Nations, Tulsa, OK, 2007.

Without question, Satan does not want you to exercise your faith and press on in the high calling of Christ Jesus. He is perfectly satisfied with you sitting on the sidelines as a spectator. And he will do whatever he can to keep you out of the game. I love the way author, counselor and speaker **John Eldredge** tackles this in his book *Wild at Heart*. He says…

> "Satan will try to get you to agree with intimidation *because he fears you*. You are a huge threat to him. He doesn't want you waking up and fighting back because when you do, he loses. 'Resist the devil,' James says, *'and he will flee from you'* (James 4:7, emphasis added). So he's going to try to keep you from taking a stand. He moves from subtle seduction to open assault. The thoughts come crashing in, all sorts of stuff begins to fall apart in your life, your faith seems paper thin.
>
> …Why does everything seem to fall apart at work when you're making some advances at home, or vice versa? Because we are at war and the Evil One is trying an old tactic—strike first and maybe the opposition will turn tail and run. He can't win, you know. As Franklin Roosevelt said, 'We have nothing to fear but fear itself.'"[10]

> Stand fast and don't allow your adversaries to terrify you.
> Be brave, strong and courageous, ready to face and deal with
> any opposition rather than withdrawing from it!
> **—John Bevere** (page 185)

> Only be strong and very courageous, that you may observe
> to do according to all the law which Moses My servant
> commanded you; do not turn from it to the right hand
> or to the left, that you may prosper wherever you go.
> **—Joshua 1:7**

PRAYER OF DELIVERANCE

Father God, for too long I have allowed the enemy to have a hold on me. I realize You paid a big price to set me free from fear and intimidation. Please forgive me for tolerating what You have liberated me from. I repent. Cleanse me with the blood of Jesus. Today is the day I choose to confront this stronghold and break free. I am seated with Christ in the heavenly places, far above all principality and power and might and dominion, and every name that is named, not only in this age but also in that which is to come. I say "No more!" I break the power of the spirit of fear and intimidation off my life right now in the name of Jesus Christ. I am free! No longer does this spirit have a hold on me! I choose now to walk in this freedom with boldness in Jesus' name!

Pen Your Progress

As we come to the close of this chapter, take some time to reflect on the truths that have been presented. Because you have chosen to *press on past* the enemy's intimidation, you are now ready to *press into* the plans God has for your life. He stands ready to strengthen you for the task. Write anything specific the Lord is showing you or asking you to do at this time.

1. Quotes on *Fear* (www.dailychristianquote.com, retrieved 9/20/08). 2. Adapted from *Noah Webster's First Edition of an American Dictionary of the English Language* (1828), Republished in facsimile edition by Foundation for American Christian Education (San Francisco, CA 1995). 3. Quotes on *Courage*, retrieved 8/8/08, see note 1. 4. See note 1. 5. See note 2. 6. Ibid. 7. Adapted from *Vine's Complete Expository Dictionary of Old and New Testament Words*, W. E. Vine (Nashville, TN: Thomas Nelson, Inc. 1996) p. 45. 8. John G. Lake, *Spiritual Hunger, The God-Men and Other Sermons* (Dallas, TX: Christ for the Nations, Inc. 1979) pp. 54, 55. 9. See note 2. 10. John Eldredge, *Wild at Heart* (Nashville, TN: Thomas Nelson Publishers, 2001) pp.166, 167.

Freedom Notes

Freedom Notes

"I hope you have learned in this series and all these lessons that fear and intimidation don't have to be any part of your life, of your home, or your ministry—that you can walk **fear-free** if you truly *fear God* and *love Him*."

—John Bevere
adapted from session 8

Freedom Notes

Freedom Notes

Freedom Notes

Freedom Notes

Freedom Notes

JOIN OVER **300,000 PEOPLE** WHOSE LIVES
HAVE BEEN TRANSFORMED BY OUR CURRICULUMS.

BREAKING INTIMIDATION
CURRICULUM

Everyone has been intimidated at some point in life. Do you really know why it happened or how to keep it from happening again? John Bevere exposes the root of intimidation, challenges you to break its fearful grip, and teaches you to release God's gifts and establish His dominion in your life.

INCLUDES:
- EIGHT 30-MINUTE VIDEO SESSIONS ON 3 DVDS
- EIGHT 30-MINUTE AUDIO SESSIONS ON 4 CDS
- BREAKING INTIMIDATION BOOK
- DEVOTIONAL WORKBOOK
- ADVERTISING POSTER

HONOR'S REWARD
CURRICULUM

This curriculum will unveil the power and truth of an often overlooked principle-Honor. If you understand the vital role of this virtue, you will attract blessing both now and for eternity. This insightful message teaches you how to extend honor to your Creator, family members, authorities and those who surround your world.

INCLUDES:
- 12 30-MINUTE VIDEO LESSONS ON 4 DVDS
- 12 30-MINUTE AUDIO LESSONS ON 6 CDS
- HONOR'S REWARD HARDBACK BOOK
- DEVOTIONAL WORKBOOK
- POSTER

DRIVEN by Eternity
CURRICULUM

Making Your Life Count Today & Forever

We were made for eternity. This life on earth is but a vapor. Yet too many live as though there is nothing on the other side. Scriptural laws and principles may be applied to achieve success on earth, but are we prepared for eternity? This power-packed teaching, including an allegory on the Kingdom of Affabel, will help you understand that the choices you make today will determine how you spend eternity.

INCLUDES:
- 12 40-MINUTE VIDEO LESSONS ON 4 DVDS
- DRIVEN BY ETERNITY HARDBACK BOOK
- HARDBACK DEVOTIONAL WORKBOOK
- AFFABEL AUDIO THEATER

CALL FOR INFORMATION
ABOUT OUR
SMALL GROUP UPGRADE

THE BAIT OF SATAN
CURRICULUM

Jesus said, "It's impossible that no offenses will come."
–Luke 17:1

A most crucial message for believers in this hour.

"This message is possibly the most important confrontation with truth you'll encounter in your lifetime. The issue of offense – the very core of *The Bait of Satan* – is often the most difficult obstacle an individual must face and overcome."

– John Bevere

INCLUDES:
- 12 30-MINUTE VIDEO LESSONS ON 4 DVDs
- 12 30-MINUTE AUDIO LESSONS ON 6 CDs
- BEST-SELLING BOOK THE BAIT OF SATAN
- WORKBOOK
- POSTER

A HEART ABLAZE
CURRICULUM

Jesus has never accepted lukewarmness. Rather, He calls for passion! This message will challenge you to exchange a mediocre relationship with God for a vibrant, fiery one.

INCLUDES:
- 12 30-MINUTE VIDEO LESSONS ON 4 DVDs
- 12 30-MINUTE AUDIO LESSONS ON 6 CDs
- A HEART ABLAZE BEST-SELLING BOOK
- WORKBOOK
- PROMOTIONAL MATERIALS

UNDER COVER
CURRICULUM

Under the shadow of the Almighty, there is liberty, provision and protection. Unfortunately, many don't understand how to find this secret place. In this curriculum you will learn how biblical submission differs from obedience. You will also learn the distinction between direct and delegated authority and how to respond to and overcome unfair treatment.

INCLUDES:
- 12 30-MINUTE VIDEO LESSONS ON 4 DVDs
- 12 30-MINUTE AUDIO LESSONS ON 6 CDs
- BEST-SELLING BOOK UNDER COVER
- DEVOTIONAL WORKBOOK
- POSTER

DRAWING NEAR
INDIVIDUAL CURRICULUM

John has specially prepared this *Drawing Near Personal Devotional Journey* to lead you into times of private and intimate communion with God. This personal devotional kit acts as a treasure map, guiding you around potential pitfalls and breaking through personal barriers.

Embark on this life-changing encounter, leading you to discover how to cultivate your intimate relationship with God.

INCLUDES:
- 12 30-MINUTE VIDEO LESSONS ON 4 DVDs
- BEST-SELLING BOOK DRAWING NEAR
- 84-DAY DEVOTIONAL
- WORKBOOK

Audio Theaters

RESCUED AUDIO THEATER

2 hours on 2 CDs

From the novel *Rescued*

Starring:
  Roma Downey from *Touched by an Angel*
  John Rhys-Davies from *The Lord of the Rings*
  Marisol Nichols from the hit TV show *24*

A trapped father. A desperate son. A clock ticking down toward certain death and a fate even more horrible still...

For Alan Rockaway, his teenaged son Jeff, and his new bride Jenny, it's been little more than a leisurely end to a week-long cruise ...a horrifying crash and even more, a plunge toward the unknown...

Everything Alan has assumed about himself is flipped upside down. In the ultimate rescue operation, life or death is just the beginning!

AFFABEL — WINDOW OF ETERNITY

2.5 hours on 4 CDs

FEATURING JOHN RHYS-DAVIES AND A CAST OF HOLLYWOOD ACTORS

AN EPIC AUDIO THEATER PORTRAYING THE REALITY OF THE JUDGMENT SEAT OF CHRIST. GET READY TO BE CHANGED FOREVER...AND PREPARE FOR ETERNITY!

This audio dramatization, taken from John Bevere's book, *Driven by Eternity*, will capture your heart and soul as you experience life on "the other side" where eternity is brought into the present and all must stand before the Great King and Judge. Be prepared for a roller coaster ride of joy, sorrow, astonishment, and revelation as lifelong rewards are bestowed on some while others are bound hand and foot and cast into outer darkness by the Royal Guard!

BOOKS BY JOHN

The Bait of Satan
Breaking Intimidation
Drawing Near
Driven by Eternity
Enemy Access Denied
The Fear of the Lord
A Heart Ablaze

Honor's Reward
How to Respond When You Feel Mistreated
Rescued
Thus Saith the Lord
Under Cover
Victory in the Wilderness
The Voice of One Crying

Messenger International
life-transforming truth.

Messenger International, founded by John and Lisa Bevere, imparts the fear of the Lord while inspiring freedom through the spoken and written Word to release people into their fulfilled lives in Christ.

UNITED STATES
P.O. Box 888
Palmer Lake, CO
80133-0888
800-648-1477 (US & Canada)
Tel: 719-487-3000
Fax: 719-487-3300
mail@MessengerInternational.org

EUROPE
P.O. Box 1066
Hemel, Hempstead HP2 7GQ
United Kingdom
In UK 0800 9808 933
Tel: +44 1442 288 531
europe@MessengerInternational.org

AUSTRALIA
P.O. Box 6200
Dural, D.C. NSW 2158
AUSTRALIA
In AUS 1-300-650-577
Tel: +61 2 8850 1725
aus@MessengerInternational.org

The Messenger television program broadcasts in 216 countries including the U.S. on GOD TV, the Australian Christian Channel and the New Life Channel in Russia. Please check your local listings for day and time.

www.MessengerInternational.org